NO NEED TO WEAR RUBBERS
THE 1925 TRAVEL DIARY OF JAMES O'NEIL

No Need to Wear Rubbers

THE 1925 TRAVEL DIARY OF JAMES O'NEIL

Edited with an introduction
and notes by his son Paul O'Neill

Copyright © Paul O'Neill

Library and Archives Canada Cataloguing in Publication

O'Neil, James, 1882-1953
  No Need to Wear Rubbers : The Travel Diary of James O'Neil /
Paul O'Neill, editor.

ISBN 0-9738501-1-6

1. O'Neil, James, 1882-1953--Travel--Europe. 2. Europe--Description and travel. I. O'Neill, Paul, 1928- II. Title.

D921.O56 2005   914.04'5   C2005-905481-6

All rights reserved. No part of this book may be reproduced or transmitted in any form or by any means - graphic, electronic, or mechanical - without the prior written permission of the publisher.

5 4 3 2 1

Front cover photo: Place de Catalunya, along the street of Grand Via de les Cortes Catalanes, Barcelona (Tourist Offices Generalitat de Catalunya)
Back cover photos: Bay de Verde

Layout & Design: Greg Merner

Printed in Canada

Boulder Publications Ltd.

Portugal Cove-St. Philip's
Newfoundland & Labrador, Canada

www.boulderpublications.ca

THIS DIARY BY MY FATHER IS PUBLISHED IN

IN REMEMBRANCE OF HIM AND OF HIS SIBLINGS:

THOMAS - 1873 (DIED IN INFANCY)

DANIEL - 1878-1952

MICHAEL - 1876-1957

ELLEN - 1880-1968

AND JAMES - 1882-1953

ALL OCCUPY FOND PLACES IN MY MEMORY

ACKNOWLEDGEMENTS

I would mainly like to thank people who helped with the notes for this book, since the diary is its own acknowledgement of a European tour that took place more than 80 years ago. My special thanks go to people and organizations that helped in preparing the work for publication. They include Helen Miller, Archivist, City of St. John's; Bert Riggs, Archivist, Centre for Newfoundland Studies; Heather Wareham, Maritime Archive – Memorial University; the Map Library at Queen Elizabeth II Library; Karen Lippold and staff of Information Services, Memorial University Library; Joel Reardon, British High Commission, Ottawa; Susi Woodhouse, MLA Government of U.K., London; Maria Lampert, British Library Research Service, London; Jacky Cowdrey, Royal Albert Hall Archives, London; the Embassy of Spain, Ottawa; Jacques-Henri Gagnon, Canadian Embassy in France, Paris; the Embassy of France, Ottawa; Tourist offices Generalitat de Catalunya, Spain; Irish National Library, Dublin; National Photographic Archive, Temple Bar, Dublin; and Ase A. Lange, Riksarkivet, Oslo, Norway. All are sincerely thanked for providing information and illustrations. I am also indebted to several friends who so generously provided material on people mentioned in the notes, especially Dr. Aidan Maloney, Derek Bowring, Michael Hope, Harry Bradshaw (Dublin), John O'Dea, Wallace Furlong, and in particular Dr. Christopher Pratt, for providing details regarding his great uncle, Art Pratt.

The fortunes of my father's diary have now stretched over more than three quarters of a century. It has been in and out of drawers, cupboards and shelves, yet remained intact with photos, theatre programs, and postcards due to my mother's care. I am certain he never even vaguely dreamed it would one day be published, let alone with notes and editing from his son. It might have become a forgotten family treasure had not Gavin Will of Boulder

Publications undertaken the task of seeing it into print. I owe him my thanks for his encouragement and assistance.

Lastly, I must acknowledge with sincere gratitude and heartfelt thanks Sheilah Roberts for the typing and research assistance provided on this project. Without her deep interest and many valuable suggestions, as well as tracking down elusive information for the notes and photo illustrations all over Europe and Canada, the task of preparing the diary for publication would have been almost impossibly onerous.

PREFACE

This book contains my father's words and observations. Little has been changed from what he wrote. Most of the editing done was purely cosmetic. Comments, for the sake of clarity, are in square brackets, while explanatory notes are at the end of the journal. The handwritten, pen-and-ink originals of the two volumes from which the diary was copied, are to go with my papers to Memorial University's Centre for Newfoundland Studies.

Before reading my father's diary I feel you should know a little of who he was and how the work found its way into print after more than three-quarters of a century. I first met James O'Neil, a merchant of Bay de Verde, in St. Clare's Hospital, St. John's, within an hour of my being born, on the afternoon of Friday, 26 October 1928. I was the firstborn of his marriage to Mary Joseph Flynn of St. John's, who was the daughter of his first cousin Mary Moore Flynn. Baptised Mary Joseph, Mary was named after a sister who died in infancy, and Joseph after her mother's favourite saint. Her family called her Josephine, while most of her friends called her Jo. My father's name for her was Joey. They had been wed in the Presentation Convent Chapel, Cathedral Square (her old school) on Candlemas Day, February 2 1928. It was foretold by the doctor in Old Perlican, near where we lived in Bay de Verde, that I would be making my first appearance in this world at the end of the first week in November. So my father and mother made the 10-hour train journey to St. John's at the beginning of the last week in October, so she could see Dr. Cluny MacPherson and make arrangements for my arrival at St. Clare's.

Since my maternal grandparent's house on Wood Street was full at the time, my parents checked into the rooming house of a friend, taximan Frank Wheeler, 47 Prince of Wales Street, close to St. Clare's Hospital. Possibly because of the ten hour, jolting

TRAVEL DIARY OF JAMES O'NEIL

Flakes such as these, upon which salted fish was dried for sale and shipment overseas, covered the waterfront in Bay de Verde until the post-war years of the 1940's. At one time it was the largest inshore fishing community in Conception Bay. The Roman Catholic Church of the Assumption stands in the background. (Provincial Archives of Newfoundland & Labrador)

train ride to the city, they barely settled in the Wheeler household when mother realized I was on the way. Frank Wheeler rushed her west on LeMarchant Road, to St. Clare's, then a wooden building standing on the corner of St. Clare Avenue. While my father waited at Wheeler's, Dr. MacPherson, inventor of the prototype of the gas masks used in World War I, delivered a charming infant boy, who, I am sure, was nine pounds of sheer joy. I know my father, who did not marry until he was 46, must have thought of me that way, when holding the infant son he never dreamed he would have.

As a young man, Jim O'Neil was working at Bowring's around the turn of the twentieth century, and boarding with his only sister, my aunt Nellie Kennedy, wife of Captain Nicholas Kennedy. When captain of Bowring's S.S. *Terra Nova*, uncle Nick was first to the rescue of those on board another of the firm's vessels, the shipwrecked *S.S. Florizel*. My aunt Nellie once told me that after my father reached 40 years of age, with only one failed romance in 1919, the family gave up all hopes of his ever marrying. Then, in 1927, when he saw his first cousin's daughter, Jo Flynn, an affable flapper, 29 years of age, again fresh from New York where she had been working as a governess with several elite families, his heart did a flip.

The skinny schoolgirl he last saw at her mother's house before she left for America was now a beautiful, sophisticated young woman with a winsome personality. She had come home to see her father, on hearing he had an eye put out by a woman in the Nickel movie theatre who missed her hat, and plunged her hatpin through his eye. Seeing her handsome cousin through mature eyes, romance blossomed. Their engagement soon followed in spite of the fact he was sixteen years her senior and her mother's first cousin. Because of the consanguinity, she had to seek the permission of Archbishop Roche of St. John's, whom she knew. His Grace told her to go ahead and marry him saying, "Josephine, you couldn't find a finer man."

TRAVEL DIARY OF JAMES O'NEIL

They honeymooned that winter at the Cochrane Hotel in St. John's. Come spring, Jim and Joey settled in Bay de Verde in the 14 room, Second Empire house that my grandfather had the Southcott firm from St. John's build in 1881-1882. My father was the first and the last O'Neil born in that house, in December 1882.

For two or three years before my arrival, Dad had been dining out on the tales of two trips he made before being snagged by matrimony. They were two years in which he ended up in undeclared bankruptcy because of a poor fishing season. In 1920, taking what little money he had left after wiping out all his debts, he went to New York. When a poor season happened again in 1925, he went to Europe on the Norwegian steamer S.S. *Agga*, laden with saltfish for Spain, which undoubtedly included some of his own. As a child, I became as spellbound by his tales about his European travels, as my mother became irritated. When I was 10, I was almost as familiar with the Riviera in Cannes, as I was with the public road in Bay de Verde. His photos, theatre programs, books of postcards, hotel bills and folders of the journey entranced me, as they did my younger brother John, and we spent many stormy days excitedly rummaging through them in the attic.

By the time I was 12, I was reading bits and pieces from his diary, and in 1948, when I was 20, badly bitten by the travel bug myself, I began my own journeying by sailing off to New York's National Academy of Theatre Arts. Within two years, performing with professional theatre companies from New York on tours, I visited almost every state in the USA. Having spent more than 66 of my 76 years reading Dad's diary, it is now with the greatest pleasure that I usher it into print. You will not find it startling, or amazing, or revealing of scandals. It is a truly fascinating account of a Newfoundland gentleman's European travels long, long ago, and my father was a gentleman in every sense of the word. I never recall seeing him without a dress shirt, tie and vest, even on hot summer days. I loved him dearly, as he was the most remarkable man I have ever known. I hope this journal of his, written more than three quarters of a century ago, will be for readers today a mirror of a time and things that were, but are no more, in this electronic age.

While fishermen called him Skipper Jim, and his brother, the father of Bishop O'Neill, called him Skipper Mike, my father's business stationary identifies him as J.F. O'Neil, General Stores and Fishery supplies - Manufacturer of Refined Cod Liver Oil, Bay de Verde, Conception Bay. To discover the man behind the name, I invite you to read and enjoy this diary.

Paul O'Neill
St. John's, Newfoundland, 2005

A photograph from the mid-1930s of James O'Neil with sons John and Paul. John (1930-1984) is on the left, Paul is on the right. A budding actor, Paul is making a face, which he did almost every time a camera was produced. The photo shows the close, loving relationship between father, sons, and brothers.

TRAVEL DIARY OF JAMES O'NEIL

THE MYSTERY OF THE SECOND "L"

In answer to a frequently asked question from friends and others, I must explain. My great grandfather, Thomas O'Neil, emigrated from Shanagarry, County Cork, Ireland in 1824, to work for Thomas Ridley in Harbour Grace. When he began in business for himself in Newfoundland in 1834, he dropped the "O" and second "L" from his name, becoming Thomas Neil, probably thinking it looked more English and would help him get ahead faster. This action resulted in the family being known as "the Nails" by people in Bay de Verde. Thomas later changed the spelling to Neale. I have several letters from the Governor of the day addressed to Thomas Neale, asking him to be on various boards, give dole to the poor, etc. My father told me that my grandfather, John, eventually dropped the "E" and restored the "O", making the spelling O'Neil. Neither he, nor my father, ever knew a second "L" was missing.

My first cousin, Bishop John M. O'Neill, who became used to having his name spelled O'Neill when studying for his Doctor of Divinity at Quebec's Laval University, adopted that spelling. In the early 1950s, he became the first member of the family in Newfoundland to visit relatives in Ireland. On his return, he told me there was an "L" missing from our name and that all our Irish relatives, living and dead, were O'Neill not O'Neil. With that information I decided to revert to the original spelling. There were only two holdouts of which I am aware. One was my brother, John, who remained O'Neil until his death. His children and grandchildren spell the name with one "L". The other is Michael O'Neil and family of Corner Brook, son of my first cousin and godfather, Dr. Brendan O'Neil of Aguathuna, brother of Bishop O'Neill.

xiii

SPAIN

February 6 (Friday), 1925

With mingled feelings of pleasurable anticipation and tingling nervousness, I boarded the Norwegian steamer S.S. *Agga*, which was loaded with dry, salt codfish, and sailed from Harvey's wharf at 8:00 pm., bound for the port of Alicante, Spain. The weather was frosty, and getting outside the heads [narrows] we found a good swell on, but my fellow passenger [Robert J. Coleman] and I, soon sought our bunks, which were two lounges [couches], in a nice cabin off the small but comfortable saloon.

This partial photo of Bay de Verde shows the location of the O'Neil premises which encompasses most of the right side of the photo from the waterfront to the large white building, upper right, excluding the Quinlan Brothers premises in the lower right corner. Following the death of my father in 1953, Maurice and Pat Quinlan, sons of his lifelong friend Patrick Quinlan of Red Head Cove, bought much of his property from my mother, including his shop. The purchase helped in launching their incredibly prosperous fishery enterprise. (George Hunter)

TRAVEL DIARY OF JAMES O'NEIL

While he was touring Europe in the late winter of 1925, this was how my father's waterfront fishing premises looked in Bay de Verde. The bottom floor contained a stage facility for processing and storing fish, while on the top floor was the bunk house for his crew of sharemen. At the back was a large room for knitting and storing twine nets. (Author's photo)

February 7 (Saturday)

Wind Northwest. Blowing strong and frosty. My companion and I are getting our sea legs. The ship is doing about nine knots per hour.

February 8 (Sunday)

The wind is still Northwest and blowing strong. We passed a steamer this morning and two others later in the day.

15

NO NEED TO WEAR RUBBERS

February 9 (Monday)

The wind is still Northwest and strong but there is a very noticeable change in the atmosphere. There is now no need for an overcoat when on deck. I spend much of my time on the bridge with nothing but the broad, turbulent Atlantic in our line of vision today.

February 10 (Tuesday)

Wind Northwest to West with half a gale blowing. I am wondering today if it is ever moderate out here on the ocean.

February 11 (Wednesday)

The winds are fairly moderate at last. However, nothing was sighted. I am now settling down to life onboard ship. I occupy most of my time with reading, sleeping, eating and talking.

February 12 (Thursday)

We are half over the road. The Captain says the Azores [Islands in the Atlantic, known by 1351 and colonized by the Portuguese in 1445] are abeam about 300 miles to the south. The wind was Westerly and strong. We have not had a head wind or seen fog since leaving port.

February 13 (Friday)

Wind Northwest again, with nothing sighted since February 8. Blowing a gale with a heavy sea running. The Captain says it's

TRAVEL DIARY OF JAMES O'NEIL

My father, seen here with his friend and traveling companion, St. John's commission merchant, Robert Coleman (left) is standing on the deck of the Norwegian ship SS Agga *as she made her way from St. John's to Alicante, Spain.* (Author's photo)

only fairly heavy, although I think differently. This is the roughest sea I have ever seen. [My father said he could never remember being seasick.] The engines have been running slow the last three days.

February 14 (Saturday)

Still a gale blowing from the North and the engines running slow. We made 150 miles in the last 24 hours in a pretty heavy sea. There have been rain and hail squalls. The sea is on the port quarter and the decks are continually awash.

17

February 15 (Sunday)

Wind N. Moderate today but big swell. Fine and warm. It is a great relief to see a calm sea and not hear the wind howling through the rigging. Expect to sight Cape St. Vincent, Portugal on Tuesday.

February 16 (Monday)

Beautiful warm day. Wind W. Light. Sea smooth at 2:00 p.m. Sighted a steamer bound east. Toward midnight saw the lights of four ships. Today is the first time we have seen a ship since February 8, and having no wireless [radio] we felt rather isolated in the interval. One can lay off in comfort on deck without an overcoat and I very much enjoy the nights on the bridge.

February 17 (Tuesday)

Fine, warm and calm. Sighted land – Cape St. Vincent at 2:15 p.m. The lighthouse here was formerly a monastery. This is our first sight of Europe. The Cape is abeam at 8:00 p.m. Eleven days from St. John's. Time is 3 hours and 56 minutes faster than Newfoundland time. During the trip I was interested in watching the daily progress of the ship on the great circle, on the chart. Many ships are in sight going to and coming from the Mediterranean. At 11:00 p.m., I came off the bridge to get a cup of coffee. There are 12 ships in sight. All on board appear in good humour as the trip was a rough one and we are getting near the end of the road.

TRAVEL DIARY OF JAMES O'NEIL

In his diary my father mentions having this photograph taken of himself and Robert Coleman (right) as they walked along the Promenade des Anglais, Nice. Note that on a very warm day, they are attired in hats, ties and vests, even when on holiday. (Author's photo)

February 18 (Wednesday)

Fine, calm and water smooth. We are passing many ships. Cape Trafalgar lighthouse in sight at 1:30 p.m. and at 2:30 p.m. Trafalgar lighthouse abeam. Trafalgar Bay of Nelson fame in full view, also the north coast of Africa. At 3:30 p.m. we are passing Tangiers, Morocco, and can see the town quite plainly. At 5:30 p.m. we are passing Tarifa[1] lighthouse and town. The houses are all one-story and very white. Gibraltar is now in sight. At 6:30 p.m. we are passing the Rock. Darkness has set in and we must content ourselves with seeing the lights of the town and the shadow of the great fortress. We expected to call at Gibraltar for coals, but on account of not arriving before night we passed on, much to my disappointment.

February 19 (Thursday)

Fine day but cold. Wind E. Water smooth. Steaming up the Mediterranean and passing numerous ships. At 7:00 a.m. we are passing the snow capped, cloud encircled, Sierra Nevada Mountains, which are 7,000 feet high, and at 10:30 a.m. the town of Almera, which reminds me forcibly of grapes, is slipping by us. Saw a steamer loading salt at San Miguel. There are no natural harbours around here and this ship was loading on a straight shore, lighters carrying off the cargo. On every headland as we bring them open there is a round stone tower. Those were used in bygone days as signal towers. Fires were lighted in them on the approach of the enemy and from tower to tower the signal fires watch. *"Cape beyond Cape, in endless range, whose twinkling points of fire."* [*The Spanish Armada* by Thomas MacCauley]

February 20 (Friday)

Got out of bunk early. This is an ideal morning, like July at home. Arrived inside the mole or sea wall of Alicante at 8:00 a.m., 13 and a half days from St. John's. The harbour is a nice sight, fairly large, but the town is rather small. Landed at 10:00 a.m. and went to the Palace Hotel, where we engaged a room at 14 pesetas each. (Exchange being 14 cents for a peseta). Saw Hawes's fish stores, which are well kept, clean and wholesome. Ruins of two old Moorish castles on the hill, one of which we visited. People have burrowed like rats under the walls of this castle and made rather primitive homes there. Part of one of the castles is used for a signal station. The cliff and rock formations are very soft and can be easily cut into. These are not at all like the rocks up north.

There are no trees and the landscape looks scorched. I was not surprised at the burnt look, when I was informed that it is not unusual to go months without rain in this warm climate. I was rather

TRAVEL DIARY OF JAMES O'NEIL

The SS Agga, *with her load of salt fish from St. John's, docked in the Mediterranean port of Alicante, on Spain's Costa Blanca. It is seen here in 1925 from the Castillo de Santa Barbara which crowns a hill dominating the city. It was here my father went ashore to begin his travels and record the diary of his trip.* (Encyclopedia Univeral)

struck with the shops with their extensive glass cases (displaying their wares) which were placed on the walls of the stores on the outside.

February 21 (Saturday)

I was informed this morning that I could not get any breakfast, as this meal has no existence in Spain, but I succeeded in getting a cup of coffee and roll. Called to see Dr. Campos (a large handler of Newfoundland fish) at his office at 9:00 a.m. At 10:30 a.m. took the train for Valencia. The railway cars here are quite small and the railway a narrow gauge. We went through many tunnels and under some high mountains. There is no going around the hills here. The policy appears to be go through them. The composition of the stone being very soft; the soil near Alicante is poor, with the consistency of mud. Met the postal official on train who spoke a

21

little English. After repeated efforts and much stammering with the unfamiliar English language he informed me that he had heard that people live in wooden houses in my country. When I answered in the affirmative, he expressed great surprise and asked me if those people were not fearful of being burnt.

Hills are barren and treeless except for some nice almond trees. I met two Americans on this train. Gardens or farms on the hillsides are perfectly level, being built up like steps of a huge stairs. This is done, I understand, to conserve and hold moisture. No timber houses of any kind to be seen, all erections are stone or stucco. Mules and donkeys are conspicuous at the railroad stations that we pass.

Nearing Valencia the fields of lemon and orange trees in orderly rows and in full bloom are a fine sight. The landscape is all green in this section. The railroad stations are piled high with oranges being assorted by women. Met a man from India on this train who spoke English fluently. He is a leather merchant at Barcelona. Arrived at Valencia at 9:00 p.m. and went to the Palace Hotel. This hotel has an orchestra. Met Englishmen there at dinner. We are paying 18 pesetas or about $2.50 a day each for room and board. Valencia railroad station is quite large, but the trains so far are rather uncomfortable.

There are soldiers fully armed and uniformed in all the railway cars; the first-class of which are made up of compartments to accommodate six adults. The hotel vans (motor driven buses) with porters and interpreters meet all trains to convey prospective guests to the hotels. Those buses also take hotel patrons to trains when they are leaving. This conveyance is charged on the guest's bills. I took a short walk after dinner and was not very favourably impressed with the little of the city which I saw. The street cars or buses are unique, as their motive power is a bevy of donkeys. This hotel has a white marble stairs and the two meals with which we are served, namely lunch and dinner, are very appetizing and the service is good.

February 22 (Sunday)

Today I saw the fish-market which was in full swing. There was a great variety of fish, vegetables, poultry, etc. Some women were busy plucking the feathers off the poultry, others dressing down fish of various kinds and several trying to induce me to buy a fish, a duck or a bunch of vegetables; but as I was paying on board at the Palace those inducements did not appeal to me. There was a regular babel of talk. Went to mass, but the congregation appeared to have little devotion. I noticed particularly that no bell was rung at the consecration and very few knelt. The church was a very nice one, with altars all round it and I was struck especially with the splendid ceiling. After mass, I visited a nice park, after which I went to a saloon for a glass of beer.

There was a pianola here with three violins in a glass case over it that played along with the pianola and was a regular orchestra. It is the first I have seen. Had a two-hour taxi drive after lunch. The sights were somewhat disappointing and as our taxi man could not make himself understood to us, we missed much of interest. It is a great drawback to be unable to speak the language of the country. We were in one building which was built in the sixth century. Taxi men charge eight pesetas an hour. We drove to the waterfront and had a good view of the harbour, which is both commodious and attractive. The warehouses are fine structures, some of them are ornamented with stained glass windows. Sculptured figures also adorn the outside walls.

The streets are narrow and the road surfaces outside the city are rough and uneven. We met many priests with their flat hats. It struck me that priests are not as highly respected here as in northern countries. Saw the carnival today, but it did not appeal to me. It is such another festival as our Christmas mummers. The streets are crowded and all are happy and evidently getting great fun out of this fête, which is an annual affair. The saloons are crowded with men, women and children. We had a glass of Johnny Walker at two pesetas. Those people are very temperate. Among all the crowds seen in the streets and cafés, no one showed signs of overindulgence in strong drink.

A gallon of the kind of beer they drink here would not intoxicate. Wines and beer are the national drinks. Only the men from the north drink Johnny Walker and kindred hard liquors.

Decided to leave by tonight's train for Barcelona. As this is winter, I notice many older men wearing heavy wool shawls. These apparently take the place of overcoats. A large percentage of women wear black and almost all the fair sex wear heavy black veils. We left for Barcelona at 8:30 p.m., our ticket costing 50 pesetas. We found it impossible to get a sleeper. Coleman slept on a lounge that went right across the full width of the train. This lounge was about 12 feet long and in the centre was a long arm or headrest. A very big señora slept on the same lounge, her feet touching Coleman's.

On the opposite end of this compartment the lounge was only long enough to hold one, as the door took quite a space. As this lounge was taken up by the senora's husband, a huge man with an exuberant growth of well-trimmed whiskers, I was forced to retire to another compartment, where, in solitary confinement, I confided myself to the arms of Morpheus. After a refreshing sleep I went back to the compartment in which I had left my companion. As I stood in the door I saw that all three were still asleep, but I noticed that the lady had tacked in her sleep and now lay with her head near Coleman's feet.

Within two minutes of my arrival, Coleman, still asleep, kicked out, or rather stretched with great force, his cramped leg and a perfect connection being made with the senora's head. She screamed and bellowed like a bull and scrambled to her feet. This

TRAVEL DIARY OF JAMES O'NEIL

A truly impressive double row of date palms line the Esplanada de España in this 1925 photo. Boats were for rent in the harbour and regular cruises went to the offshore island of Tabarca. The Costa Blanca itself is today one large continuous resort and a favourite playground for tourists. (Spanish National Tourist Office)

violent outburst caused the other two occupants to bolt upright and confusion reigned, as none of the three knew exactly what had happened. With great difficulty to suppress my feelings and after much sign making on my part, the Spaniards and ourselves not having a mutual language, I at last explained to the satisfaction of that much excited couple what had happened and peace was restored. We came right round by the seashore of the Mediterranean and the dawn was beautiful.

February 23 (Monday)

In the early morning, with the night dew still glistening in the sun, it was a feast for the eyes to gaze on the splendidly kept gardens and farms. They were as level as a floor, divided and laid out with wonderful precision. We passed some rather nice little towns, one of which named Gava, at which we arrived at 7:40 a.m., had its railroad station in a nice little park with an abundance of beds of many coloured flowers.

NO NEED TO WEAR RUBBERS

Arrived at Barcelona at 8:30 a.m. and went in the hotel van to the Regina Hotel. This hotel also has an orchestra. Our room and board was 20 pesetas each for double room with private bath and shower. After partaking of a light breakfast, we paid a visit to S. Cook and Sons office and later visited a Roman Catholic Cathedral which was consecrated in 1058. It was very dark in there, as the windows were just mere slits in the walls. It would scarcely be possible to read there without artificial light. The altars are enclosed behind a very heavy fence made of iron rods with iron gates, and the priest who officiates always comes out armed with a heavy key. I understand the fence is there to prevent robbers from plundering the costly ornaments from the altars.

This modern electric train is on its way from Barcelona to the French border. In 1925 my father's steam train also passed this shoreline, characterized by quaint seafaring towns, charming coves lapped by crystal-clear waters, rocky cliffs and sandy shores battered at will by the Mediterranean Sea. (Turespaña)

This is a very busy town and is the second largest in Spain. I have seen a strikingly large number of priests on the street. A light breakfast of coffee and rolls is served at the Regina Hotel. Lunch from 12:00 noon to 2:30 p.m. consists of entrées (which are very good) and of great variety: soup, fish, chicken, vegetables, ice cream, fruit, biscuits, cheese and coffee.

At 2:30 p.m. started on a sightseeing tour. Visited the Arc de Triomf park [the arch, which had been built in Barcelona for the 1888 Universal Exposition, was used as the main entrance], harbour front, bull ring and churches. Bullfights, for which Spain is famous, start on March 1, and as we shall be leaving Spain before that time we shall not experience the pleasurable, or perhaps the opposite, feeling of witnessing them.

During our ramble of the city we got astray, but succeeded in getting back to the hotel at 7:00 p.m. Had dinner at 8:30 p.m. and attended grand opera at the Liceu Theatre [Grand Theatre of the Lyceum], which is the principal theatre of the city. Tickets in the dress circle [first gallery in a theatre where evening dress was once required] are 12 pesetas. The music and singing was certainly of a high order. The ladies of the audience were wonderfully dressed, but on the whole did not appear to me to be particularly attractive. Most of the ladies are inclined to be too fat. Very few señoritas had bobbed hair and none of the singers, but many young men sported bald heads. The theatre was rather elaborate with five balconies or boxes in height. The scenery is quite attractive; the sky in one scene being very well imitated, with the clouds rolling by. There was an excellent orchestra, as was to be expected in the opera house of Barcelona, beautiful paintings on the ceilings and all frescoes and ornaments on the fronts of the balconies were gilded. The name of the opera was *La Walkarie*.[2] It finished at 12:30 a.m.

On coming in the street we found it crowded with pedestrians, motor cars and streetcars. The saloon, restaurants and some of the stores are still open for business. I have yet to see a Spaniard under the influence of liquor. The weather is fine, in fact we have had no rain since leaving Newfoundland. In the morning and evening one needs a light overcoat. Soldiers are very much in evidence in the streets and there is a wonderful variety of multicoloured uniforms. It appears to me that a large percentage of the Spanish males are uniformed government officials. I noticed the Liceu Theatre was guarded by soldiers during last night's performance. The display of wonderfully coloured and rich looking mantillas, worn by the lady performers and the ladies of the audience in the theatre last night, was dazzling.

February 24 (Tuesday)

Went by car and up an almost perpendicular railway to Tibidabo.[3] This is a famous summer resort – the Coney Island of Barcelona. It is situated 1775 feet [512 metres] above the city. From here one has an excellent view of Barcelona with its surroundings – also the sea. As this is winter, it is very cold up here. There is a hotel and restaurant here, but patronage now is nil. Behind Tibidabo, in full view, is Montserrat's snowy mountains. In the afternoon, we went to a cabaret or vaudeville show. There was no entrance fee, but patrons were expected to purchase drinks at higher prices, of course, than the regular. One just sat at his table, sipped his wine, and enjoyed the show. *Eden Concert* the show was named.

On the way from here to the hotel we found the streets blocked with people. One could scarcely expect to see greater crowds or congestion in New York. This is the last day of the carnival or Mardi Gras here. Motor cars, cabs, buses and trucks are filled with girls and young men, the youth and beauty of the city, in holiday

TRAVEL DIARY OF JAMES O'NEIL

One of the most interesting places in Barcelona is the Sagrada Familia – Church of the Holy Family, designed in the Catalan style by Antoni Gaudí, known as the pride of Barcelona early in the twentieth century. The church he designed is still far from finished and will perhaps never be completed. It is beyond doubt the most extravagant fancy ever conceived in ecclesiastical architecture. (Turespaña)

Plaça de Espanya is marked by two large Venetian towers that lead to the Magic Fountain. On summer nights this fountain becomes a giant spectacle of light, water, colour and music from the end of June to the end of September. On the hill in the distance is the famous Tibidabo. The mountain is crowned by the church of el Sagrat Cor and a theme park. (Turespaña)

attire participating in the parade. Some of the ladies dressed in rich costumes of silks, satins, etc. ride in cars richly adorned and caparisoned with beautiful draperies. The onlookers busy themselves buying flowers at the numerous flower stalls and throwing them to the occupants of the vehicles. The streets are therefore strewn with flowers and confetti is flying in all directions. All appear remarkably happy.

The stores keep open at night and the electric signs are very good. There is but one subway here, but others are being excavated now. Spent an interesting hour in the market, where we saw a splendid display of fruit, vegetables and food of all kinds. It strikes me that being foreigners, or Americans, as we have been called, we are being overcharged at every possible opportunity, as an instance, last night we went to the Liceu Theatre and asked for tickets in the balcony. They sold us tickets in the dress circle, which are about the most expensive seats. Tonight we attended the Eldorado Theatre, a vaudeville show and a good one. We asked for tickets in the balcony, but again we were sold dress circle seats at six pesetas. This show did not begin until about 10:00 p.m. Dinner time here is from 8:30 p.m. to 9:30 p.m., which accounts for the late hours that the Theatre perform. At 1:00 a.m., we got back from the Eldorado.

Dramas or movie shows are not very interesting to us, as we do not know the language. This show had good music and good acrobats. One man held two other men on a stick on his shoulder fully 40 feet above the stage. A girl held on with her legs and swung three men together. A contortionist, a man who emerged from and got back into a box about the same size and shape as a 50 pound tea chest, was the best of his kind I have ever seen. A girl performer sang in very good English "Everybody's shimmeying now," and at her request a sprinkling of English-speaking men in the audience joined in.

The mantilla again attracted me, as did the beautiful rings and long earrings which adorned the ladies. Many men wore two and three large rings. There are greater crowds on the streets and in the cafés at 1:00 a.m. in the morning than one would see at the lakeside in St. John's on Regatta Day. Covered wagons and spirited horse are in evidence in the streets. The carnival revellers were still going strong as we came home at 1:00 a.m., and we passed cars, cabs, etc. banked with flowers taking part in the parade.

MARSEILLES

February 25 (Wednesday)

Ash Wednesday. Left hotel in morning and went to [Arenys de Mar] railroad station and at 10:00 a.m. left by train for Marseilles. Our bill at the Regina Hotel for two days – including wines, clothes pressed, also breakfast the third day with a nice basket of lunch for the train – was 72 pesetas each. It is raining this morning, the first we have had since we left home. This train is a good one. Our compartment takes six passengers. There's a hallway along the full length of the car on one side and cabins off the hallway. Soldiers with guns, swords and dirks still accompany us. They, like the police, wear long capes. The coal used on the train is, to me, peculiar. It is made in blocks the shape of bricks and piled in neat bulks on the tender.

We crossed the Spanish frontier into France at Cerbère Station at 12:30 p.m. We had to produce our passports several times here. Money changers join the train here whose business is to change your pesetas into francs; in other words, to buy your Spanish money from you and give you French in exchange. Shortly after leaving Cerbère we see the snow capped Pyrenees Mountains in the distance. The land along the railway from Barcelona is all

TRAVEL DIARY OF JAMES O'NEIL

A fascinating walk my father took in Barcelona began at the Place de Catalunya where the nude statue of a lady graces the pool of the fountain. Beneath the trees, left, are six more statues. Along the street of Grand Via de les Cortes Catalanes, which begins at the fountain, are some of the cities most characteristic neo-gothic structures. (Tourist Offices Generalitat de Catalunya)

taken up with attractive homes and farms and is very level.

Changed to a French train at Frasion and on going into a compartment we met an Austrian salesman whose home was in Vienna and who spoke English, French and Spanish, as well as his own language. He was on his way to Marseilles, so we went along together and found him good company. Arrived at Marseilles at midnight and as the hotels are very much crowded due to the city's close proximity to the riviera, which was then in the height of

33

its tourist season, we found it hard to get a room at a hotel. We took a taxi and after some trouble and with the help of our Austrian friend, who incidentally was a Mason, we finally secured a room at the Hotel L'amour et Paix at 45 francs each for room only. After registering at the hotel, we went out to a café or saloon and had a whiskey and soda. Our Austrian friend accompanied us and for three Black and White whiskeys and sodas and sandwiches we paid 25 francs and a 5 franc tip, about $1.50. Retired at 2:00 a.m. Also it was 2:00 a.m. when we got to bed at Barcelona the previous night.

February 26 (Thursday)

Beautiful morning. Hotels and streets packed with people. It is evident many tourists are here. Went to Cook's, who were our bankers, and were told that it was practically impossible to get a room in a hotel in any of the towns on the Riviera. The L'amour et Paix (Love and Peace) is a good hotel. The appointments are very comfortable. The walls and ceilings of the drawing and dining room are carved and nicely finished with paintings. Many guests here are English. This is the second largest city in France and its largest seaport. Its population is about 800,000 and it's a very lively spot. Had a nice walk and had lunch with our Austrian friend, afterwards going to a café for coffee and cognac. The girls are very lavishly painted and rouged.

Bought a ticket at Cook's for an afternoon tour of the city. During those tours, which are made by bus, our interpreter or lecturer, who comes along, describes all points of interest as the tour proceeds. Interesting buildings, etc., are entered. In this way the stranger within the gates of the city gets his first impressions, which I might say I found of great advantage in later expeditions. It is usual to have people of but one nationality in each car. If two nationalities are in the same car, the interpreter must speak in the language of both parties, which is a bit annoying. Left Cook's for the tour at 1:00 p.m. We visited, among other interesting places, the Roman Catholic Cathedral (not yet completed) which has cost to date 18 million francs and much more is needed to finish it.

Visited Notre Dame de la Garde, a church dedicated to soldiers and sailors, which stands on a high, almost perpendicular cleft, reached by a funicular railway. The church is beautifully finished in mosaic. Many swords, paintings, medals, etc., are hung on the walls, presented by relatives of deceased soldiers and sailors. The tower of the church is surmounted by a brightly gilded statue of the Blessed Virgin of immense size and height, which shines like gold in the sun and is plainly visible from almost any part of the city and far out to sea. Perched as it is on this church, which itself crowns this lofty crag, it looks almost as if it were suspended from the sky.

The view of the city and harbour from here is very fine. The sidewalks of this city – in some places also in the Spanish cities – have arcades over them, underneath which, in some cases, chairs and tables are placed that are used as extensions of the cafés behind them. One may walk through those cafés going along the street. There is a continual din of motor horns in the street on which our hotel is located.

Dinner starts here at 7:00 p.m. This is one and a half hours earlier than in Spain. Marseilles is not as gay a city as Barcelona. Attended a variety show tonight. The Frenchmen are well set up, healthy and smart looking. The girls in general are good looking, but paint, powder and lipstick play a large part in their make-up. Many girls have black blotches or moles on their faces. I thought they were disfigurements, as to me they looked very unsightly and I was quite surprised to learn that those blotches or moles had been put on for adornment. The predominant colour of ladies' hose is flesh colour and many of the girls wear broad leaf hats. There is not any doubt that a very large percentage of the mademoiselles here buy their complexions at the drug stores.

Marseilles, as it looked to my father in 1925. It was from here that bands of men and women marched to Paris in 1792, influencing the outcome of the French Revolution. Crowning the hill behind the great commercial port is the church of Notre Dame beloved by French sailors. The city is built on a narrow strip between two great rivers, the Rhone and Saône. (Educational Book Co.)

February 27 (Friday)

Good Friday. Visited churches, museum and zoological gardens. Saw a Gloria Swanson picture in the afternoon. Had Benedictine today at two francs a glass. I am still surprised at the sobriety of the Spanish and French. The cafés are filled with men and women drinking very light wines and beers, some are drinking café au lait or coffee and milk. Fifty per cent of the beverages consumed here are in my opinion not stronger than the Haig Ale made in New-foundland.

Cook's office was a busy spot today. About 15 officials work in the branch here. We wired our Austrian friend at Nice yesterday asking him if he could engage a room for us there. Had a wire today saying everything arranged. Dinner at the hotel tonight cost about $1.50.

We are paying 45 francs a day each for our room only. Tips are a nuisance. Usually one gives 10 per cent as a tip. We have had but two slight showers of rain since leaving Newfoundland. It is very warm today.

THE RIVIERA

February 28 (Saturday)

Left Marseilles at 9:00 a.m. (They count up to 24:00 in France beginning at midnight). The scenery along the railway from here to Nice is beautiful. This is the garden of Europe. A wonderful variety of vegetation meets the eye in all directions. The country is hilly. In some places we passed close to the shores of the Mediterranean with its surface today as smooth as glass. The sun pouring down on this peaceful sheet of blue water made a pretty picture. There are beautiful bungalows and residences, extending from the seashore, high up in the hills. Many houses have gable roofs and are covered with some sort of semicircular red brick tiles, which ingenious covering is, to say the least, quite picturesque.

The Riviera, as far as I have yet seen, is one immense park, an ever-changing panorama, practically right along. The natural tropical beauty coupled with the highly cultivated; also the many coloured and artistic homes against the verdure of the hillsides and the deep blue of the sea form a pretty picture, and one not soon to be forgotten by a visitor from the frozen north. We arrived at Nice at 1:30 p.m. We are paying 85 francs each for room with bath and meals. After lunch I walked alone (I might say relations between Coleman and I are somewhat strained) down to the seashore and had a hike on the Promenade des Anglais (English Promenade). I saw Turks in native costume selling rugs and tapestries, also many invalids were there. Crowds of tourists were lolling round on the sands or bathing in the inviting waters. I listened to a band concert in the park. There were about 50 instruments. As I was lying off in a comfortable chair enjoying the concert, the surroundings and the warm sunshine, Coleman accidentally met me and together we went to the jetty on which a large building is erected on iron props over the ocean. This is the casino or gambling hall of Nice. The principal game played appears to be roulette. Beside the gaming table there are a restaurant and café in the building, also a dance hall where dancers appear to be tripping the light fantastic, continually.

The theatre and restaurant would probably accommodate about 1,500 or more. The music is good and the place well patronized. Entrance fee is two francs. On the Promenade, which is overrun with photographers, Coleman and I had a picture taken. I paid 10 francs today for a tin of Prince Albert tobacco. Had dinner at the hotel, but was disappointed with the menu and service. The name of this hotel is the Splendid, but I fear the name is not applicable to the meals served here.

It is raining tonight. At the Café de Paris we met our Austrian friend and with him paid another visit to the gambling hall on the jetty. The limit here is 2 francs when playing Roulette and 6,000 francs or 300 dollars when playing baccarat. Old and young, women and men were sitting round the tables and playing. The girls are smoking here and they look good enough to eat, but again it's the drugstore complexions.

March 1 (Sunday)

Went to mass and almost lost a Cook's tour for which we bought tickets yesterday. The mass we attended was the children's mass. Collection was taken up by the priest. The nuns were in attendance with the girls and a priest was in charge of the boys. Girls and boys said their prayers together and aloud. Did not see any

Monte Carlo looking across from Monaco. This Mediterranean enclave within southeast France consists of three adjoining communities, Monaco (the capital), La Condamine (business district), and the fashionable gambling resort of Monte Carlo, playground of movie stars and the wealthy. (Paul O'Neill)

painted faces in the church, but I noticed the confessionals are open, where the penitent kneels, not closed like at home. The priest only is closed in. Our tour was to start at 9:15 a.m. We did not find a church until 9:00 and, as this is the first Sunday of Lent, the pastoral letter was read.

Arrived at Cook's office (which is open here on Sunday) at 10:15 a.m. The bus had been detained for us, so we jumped onboard and away to go. There were 14 passengers, with a lecturer and a chauffeur. Our fare was 40 francs each for a 78 mile drive. The country we passed through was very hilly. Our tour took us to the Maritime Alps. There were almost perpendicular mountains above and bottomless and yawning gorges below, as we motored upward. The road was so crooked that driving much of the jour-

The casino at Monte Carlo is one of the world's most famous gambling resorts. It stands on the shore with its back to the Mediterranean. In its day it drew millionaires from around the world. The wealthy still come here, but it also attracts gambling afficionados from all levels of society. (Paul O'Neill)

ney we could scarcely see more than 30 or 40 feet ahead. It was just cut out of the side of the mountain in many places, whereas in others, it was built up.

At some spots we passed, we could look straight down into canyons hundreds of feet deep with raging torrents running into them. There were picturesque and medieval villages every few miles and homes were built up in the hills and on crags in all directions. This was a one-way road – very narrow, though quite smooth – and our car, which was quite long, had sometimes to be backed up to get round a curve. When we got to our destination, a village named St. Martin de Vestibule, we were 3,160 feet above sea level. There was a thin covering of snow over the village road and plenty of it above us in the Alps. Had lunch at the Hotel de la Régence, a small roadside inn, and we afterwards had a snowball fight with the villagers. The drive was rather a cold one. Where we had lunch there was no whiskey to warm the inner man, but plenty of wine and beer. On the way back to Nice we stopped at an inn and I had a glass of hot rhum (pretty rotten stuff it was) which cost five francs.

I have not had a cup of tea since leaving the ship and not much there. No soup has been served at any hotel so far, in France. Got back to Nice at 5:00 p.m. Visited the jetty (casino) again tonight, but no luck. Many stores are open today, although it is Sunday and along the route of our tour we passed many people working.

In our car today we passed through a tunnel 900 hundred feet long under a rather high mountain. The headlights were switched on while we were going through. I have not been fed so well in the French hotels as in the Spanish. After dinner I went out alone and walked to the seaport of Nice (Villa France) along the promenade. The harbour is snug and quite safe, enclosed by sea walls. There is quite a bit of a sea on tonight. On my way back I dropped into a circus. It was fairly good and was out at midnight. I lost my way after leaving the circus, but after some time found the jetty, went in, lost a few francs, then back to the hotel and bed. It is raining quite freely. Tonight I saw a drunken man. He was a man-o-war sailor and is the first man I have seen under the influence of liquor since I left Newfoundland. The temperature here today is 57º F.

March 2 (Monday)

Rain today. I did not leave the hotel during the forenoon. We get a reduction of 10 francs at the hotel for every regular meal we do not participate in. After dinner we went to a variety show. A troop from Lyons performed. The lighting effects on the stage

NO NEED TO WEAR RUBBERS

In his diary, my father mentions being at the bridge on the Riviera between France and Italy. This picture of me standing on that bridge, with Italy just a few feet away, was taken on a visit to Menton, April 14, 1952, while on my way with friends to Athens, Greece. (Paul O'Neill)

were better than any I have ever seen. The actresses were practically nude. A United States warship arrived at the port today and in one café, which I visited after the show, those U.S. sailor boys were having a whale of a time.

The weather is still bad. When we arrived on Saturday it was glorious. There are many hotels here. The principal business is catering to tourists, many of whom come here for the winter in order to escape the rigours of the north, while others come to seek health. Some of the cafés and dance halls remain open all night. One meets many groups of strolling players, singers and dancers on the street.

March 3 (Tuesday)

Rain in the morning. Went to Cook's at 10:00 a.m. and took a car for Menton. We had but six passengers with an interpreter and chauffer, at 25 francs for return tickets. We went by the upper Grand Corniche, driving through magnificent, hilly country. To Menton is about 30 miles. We passed an old Roman village which, with its fort, was built in 50 BC. It is now in ruins. It appears as if we are driving through a park with plenty of variety to the scenery. An altitude of 1,800 feet was the highest we attained. At first there was a thin veneer of snow on the road. Orange, olive and lemon trees line the way in many places.

The city of Nice, with its jetty extending into the sea seen from the heights, forms a pretty picture. We passed the observatory and many quaint villages with their red roofed and white or cream houses. Those houses look very nice against the many coloured landscape. From the heights, we could see quite plainly below us the principality of Monaco and Monte Carlo. Arrived at Menton at 12:30 p.m. and stopped at a restaurant for lunch.

Met unexpectedly J.A. Paddon, Manager of the Bank of Montreal, St. John's, Newfoundland, at this restaurant. He just dropped in to have a drink and was glad to meet us. We joined him in a glass. He is staying in Menton at the Hotel Anglais paying 200 francs a day, which includes meals. Had a good six-course lunch for 18 francs. After lunch, visited Hotel Anglais or English Hotel. Nearly all the guests are English speaking. Joined the bus and drove to the Italian border at Pont-St. Louis. There we met the Italian guards and soldiers. There is a bridge here on which we found Italians with stands erected selling souvenirs. There is an Italian Customs House at one end of the bridge and a French Customs House on the other.

Made some purchases of cameos, etc. and after a half-hour stay, we boarded the bus for the famous or infamous city of Monte Carlo, where we had a two hour stop. This is the great gambling city whose reputation is worldwide. We visited the Casino, which is the gambling resort. Admission fee was five francs, with a half franc for getting your hat and coat checked. The latter was compulsory. There were approximately 500 or 600 present when we entered. Gaming tables were systematically placed. At some of which the lowest amount one could play was 10 francs, at others 20 francs. The sky appeared to be maximum. Young, middle aged, as well as old and decrepit men and women were gambling. Some of the players had a haunted or anxious look. Haggard and dissipated faces eagerly watched the spinning ball and registered disappointment or pleasure as the elusive ball came to a halt.

It was interesting to walk among the tables and scan the faces and also to watch the skill of the croupiers, as they gathered in the dough. A feeling of subdued excitement pervaded the place. The building is a very elaborate one inside and out and stands in a nice park. There were guards and attendants in plenty in all directions. Leaving Monte Carlo, we motored through the city of Monaco and passed quite near the prince's palace. The two cities are practically one, the dividing line being a bridge. Monaco has a nice harbour, protected by sea walls. The Duke of Westminister's four-mast yacht was moored there as we passed. Monaco, including Monte Carlo, is an independent principality of only eight square miles adjoining the south of France.

On the journey back to Nice, we came by the Lower Corniche Road and skirted the sea winding in and out along the beautiful beaches, bays and headlands and beneath towering clifts and olive groves.

Approaching Nice we came to the town of Villa France, with its beautiful mole harbour [a structure serving as a breakwater] and its multi-coloured houses grouped on the tree and flower bedecked hills. Here is situated the Duke of Connaught's[4] winter residence, with its blue roof and extensive dimensions. Arrived at Nice at 6:00 p.m. After dinner at the hotel, we went to a show. The meals at this hotel are not at all good. I might mention that guests at the hotels in Spain and France invariably have their bottle of wine or beer for lunch and dinner.

March 4 (Wednesday)

Fine morning. Taxied to aerodrome and flew for 20 minutes. Went down by way of the sea coast as far as San Remo in Italy and returned inland. This was my first experience in the air and it was quite enjoyable. As the aeroplane was an open one, I was provided with a long leather coat and cap, also a pair of flier's glasses to protect the eyes. This thrill cost me 75 francs. The sun around noon was very hot. Thousands are on the promenade, which incidentally is a concrete sidewalk about 30 feet wide and 18 miles long. After lunch, took a bus ride into the hills above Nice. Stopped at restaurants or cafés up there for refreshments. I paid five francs for a glass of whiskey. The whiskey glasses are very small and few take this beverage – those who do so take a very small one. We usually order a double glass.

We rode through lemon and orange groves. The roads are good but narrow and are one-way roads. The turns are many and sharp. Saw a man in one mountain village with a mule harnessed to a covered wagon. This wagon was fitted with drawers and compartments and was a miniature general store where one may buy [assorted items] from a water bucket to a hair comb. In three or four places, we passed by on the roadside religious statues enclosed in little cases with glass fronts and surrounded by crosses. Those were relics of former days and the first I had seen in France.

Dinner and service tonight at the Hotel Splendid was so bad that I left the table in disgust. Paid another visit to the jetty. Some were playing for rather stiff stakes tonight. I lost 30 francs and quit. The Negresco Hotel on the Promenade appears to be one of the swellest here. It has a splendid appearance, all spotlessly white outside.

March 5 (Thursday)

Spent morning on the Promenade which, with its thousands of pleasure and health seekers, presented a very gay and animated appearance. There were some splendidly dressed women and fine looking men lolling in the sun. The latest and swellest styles are in evidence here. Many were enjoying a bath in the blue waters, while hundreds sat on the beaches and sands. The bathing suits are rather abbreviated. Chairs are for hire and men are selling all sorts of things. Went to Cook's today and bought a ticket for Paris. Am leaving here at 3:00 p.m. tomorrow, and if I go right through without stopping off, I shall arrive at Paris at 10:00 a.m. Saturday.

Relations have become so strained between Coleman and I that the Riviera is not sufficiently large to hold both of us at the one time, so we have, wisely I think, decided to separate.[5] Coleman leaves tomorrow for Genoa in Italy. The third class fare (there is no second) from here to Paris is 218 francs. The ticket is good for a stop off at any stations en route and its time limit is 60 days. At 2:00 p.m. I took a Cook's bus to Cannes.

This is a fine day, and I enjoyed the drive in the open car, in which are 14 passengers with a lecturer. Passed through the town of Antibes. Airships that make this their base serve the Island of Corsica. There is a wonderfully well-preserved ancient Roman fort here. Cannes is about 35 miles from Nice. Ticket and return cost 20 francs.

This is the yachting centre of the Riviera and there is such a variety of yachts. To one born of the sea, they are both beautiful and fascinating. Saw one able-looking, three-masted Turkish yacht here with her Turkish crew in uniform. Her white enamelled sides and polished brass fittings were glistening in the sun. There were sail and power yachts of all sizes and colours. Many were varnished light and dark oak colours and some of the powerboats were very swift. Saw many windjammers under sail and powerboats speeding in the offing.

Overhead, a mile or more of the main street was thickly decorated with coloured electric bulbs, some of them in many-coloured, waterproof magic lanterns. There was to be a big festival here today and tonight, "The Battle of the Flowers," another name for the Mardi Gras or Carnival, which we saw at Barcelona. However, it is postponed until March 12.

The population is about 30,000 or 40,000 and the Carleton appears to be the principal hotel. Many wealthy people of England, America and other nations have winter homes here. I might say that Cannes is a popular resort of Sir Edgar Bowring. The extensive parking places here (for cars) were blocked. Returning to Nice, we passed a bad smash. Two cars had collided, but I don't know if there were casualties.

Johnny Walker whiskey is extensively advertised on signboards along the main thoroughfares. This advertising, of course, is for the benefit of tourists, as Frenchmen have not the slightest interest in this product of the canny Scott, a glass of which costs six francs. Arrived back at Nice at 7:00 p.m. After dinner, I enjoyed a nice walk and at 11:00 p.m. I wended my way to the Café de Paris. Scores of American sailors from a warship, which had arrived at Villa France, were there and they were having a wild time with the French lasses. Left the Café at 1:30 a.m. for the hotel. Everything was in full swing at the café when I left at that late hour.

March 6 (Friday)

Fine and warm. Spent the forenoon on the Promenade and in the jetty. The dress, or rather undress of the females, I found stunning. After lunch, I took the hotel bus to the station and at 3:00 p.m. I said goodbye to Coleman (who was at the station to take a train for Genoa at 3:15) and I joined the express for gay Paris. I was now on my own for the first time and felt somewhat nervous. Up to now, I had been with Coleman who was almost a perfect guide, the present being his eighteenth trip to Europe. From Nice to Marseilles, I travelled right round by the sea and from Marseilles up through the heart of France through Lyons, Dijon, etc. The scene here was entrancing, as the sunset came on. Compartments in those railway cars hold eight passengers, also hot and cold water are on tap. I did not meet any who spoke English. This train, being an express, stops at only a few stations. I had lunch at the restaurants in the railway stations I passed through.

TRAVEL DIARY OF JAMES O'NEIL

This cover from the 1924-25 theatre season at the Casino de Paris is typical of its time. It expresses the carefree elegance of the 1920s, when gentlemen attending the famous music hall did so in evening dress and bejeweled ladies wore sumptuous clothes. (Casino de Paris)

Casino de Paris

Léon VOLTERRA Directeur

BONJOUR PARIS!

Revue en 2 Actes et 45 Tableaux
de MM ALBERT WILLEMETZ,
SAINT-GRANIER et Jean LE SEYEUX

SAISON 1924-1925

PRIX 1 FR. 50

This page from the Casino de Paris program for 1924-25 announces the show my father saw, BONJOUR PARIS! Revue en 2 Actes et 45 Tableaux. *To have taken part in 45 tableaux must have demanded a great deal of time and energy from the performers.* (Casino de Paris)

TRAVEL DIARY OF JAMES O'NEIL

PARIS

March 7 (Saturday)

Arrived at Paris 9:40 a.m. No hotel buses are at the railway station here. I tried to hire a taxi-man to take me to the Hotel Burgundy (a small hotel which Cook's office at Nice had recommended), by shouting in my best French "Hotel Burgundy," but all those whom I tried looked puzzled and apparently asked me a question. Since I know no French I could not answer. The end result was the taxi-men left me. I had solicited so many taxi-men, all of whom had retorted with the same question, that I learnt their question, which sounded like "kel ru." I had a book in my pocket which I bought in Nice that translated French to English and vice versa.

After depositing my grips on the sidewalk so that they would not be pinched by Paris Apaches, I sat on them (the grips), withdrew my book from my pocket and after some time found that a term which sounded like "kel ru" was there and it meant "What street?" As Cook's in Nice did not give me the address of the Burgundy Hotel, I could get no help from that quarter. Suddenly, a bright thought struck me. I called a taxi-man, shouted "Thomas Cook" and away we went to a Cook's office, where I was given the necessary directions and was deposited at the Burgundy at 35 francs for room only.

In the afternoon, I went on a tour of the city with Cook's. The car took 22 passengers with lecturer and chauffeur at 25 francs. Saw quite a bit of Paris, including the stock exchange, post office and Ste. Chapel. This latter building was erected in 1243 to house the true cross. It is no longer a chapel, but is a great national monument. We were in the rooms where the King and his family assisted at the mass, with just a small hole in the wall to see the celebrant. We also saw the place on the same floor, where the nobles attended. The public worshipped downstairs in another chapel. The stained glass windows here are among the finest in the world. They were removed and stored during the Great War, fearing they may be destroyed. Adjoining are the law courts, which were included on the tour. This building was once the palace of the kings of France.

The courts were many times partly destroyed during the different revolutions, but the chapel was not once injured. Saw many gowned women lawyers. The world-renowned Dreyfus[6] trial took place here. Saw the Concierge Prison where Marie Antoinette, the last queen of France, spent 72 days until she was beheaded. Stood by the arch under which the unfortunate queen passed on her way to her execution. The lecturer also called our attention to five large flat stones in the street on which the Guillotine used to stand. Saw Marshall Ney's monument,[7] which is erected where he died, also visited the Panthéon de la Guerre. This was formerly a Roman Catholic Church, but like others it is now a national monument or museum.

The Panthéon, which is a circular building, contained a wonderful painting. The canvas which is one piece, 450 feet long and 42 feet high, covers the walls right round and stretches from floor to ceiling. There is a separate square allotted to every nation, large or small, that took sides with the allies in the Great War. In the English square for example, we have the King, Prince of Wales, leaders in the army like Kitchener,[8] etc., leaders in the navy like Admiral Jellico,[9] etc., also soldiers, nurses, guns, etc., and all life size. The picture is known as the grand panorama of the war.

We spent some time in Notre Dame Cathedral. There are three stained glass windows in this church, which were also removed during the war. The hats of the cardinals who have died belonging to this church still hang here. The interior finish of the church

The enchanting and fabulous Mlle. Mistinguett was the most famous music hall star in France between the two great wars. The man who frequently shared the spotlight with her, the legendary Maurice Chevalier, said of Mistinguett, "She is Paris!" (Casino de Paris)

was not very attractive. It was started in the twelfth century and took 100 years to complete. Its exterior is very striking and viewed from a little distance it is a noble pile.

Saw where the German shell from Big Bertha[10] struck the church of St. Gervais on Good Friday 1918, killing 80 and wounding 118. We later paid a flying visit to the cemetery where the great actress Sarah Bernhardt and that bird-like singer Adelina Patti are buried. We drove through the tough section of Paris and some of the people we saw had hard looking faces. Passed several butcher shops with gilded horses heads over the doors. In those stores nothing but horse meat is sold, but it was splendidly dressed and looked quite appetizing. After dinner, I got my first glimpse of the gay city by night, and as I wended my way through strange streets there was plenty to occupy my attention. The never ceasing crowds, the stores whose display of finery beggar description, the cafés, electric signs and the wonderfully dressed women were, I think, what struck me most on my first night.

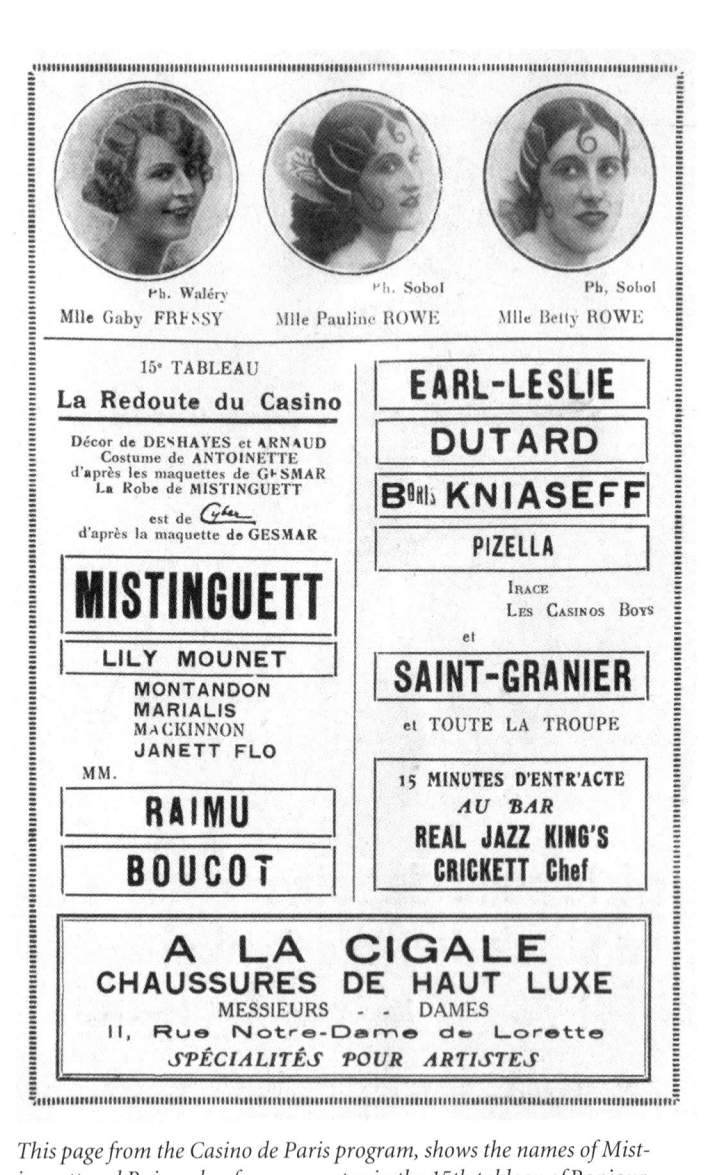

This page from the Casino de Paris program, shows the names of Mistinguett and Raimu, her famous co-star in the 15th tableau of Bonjour Paris! *Raimu is remembered today as one of the stars of Marcel Pagnol's famed French film trilogy,* César, Marius *and* Fanny. (Casino de Paris)

TRAVEL DIARY OF JAMES O'NEIL

March 8 (Sunday)

Attended 8:00 a.m. mass at the Church of the Madeline. A man in uniform, brass buttons, scarlet vest, breeches and three cornered hat, and with a brass staff in his hand (who I think is called the Major Domo), preceded the priest who took up the collection. An old woman, who looked very poor, also collected. I don't know why. Perhaps it was for herself.

After mass, I had a walk which was very enjoyable. The shop windows were a great attraction for me on this hike. At 11:00 a.m. I joined a Cook's tour to Versailles and Malmaison. In Versailles, we visited the palace of the last king of France, Louis XVI. The palace, with its beautiful grounds, its three mile long artificial lake, and its fountains, is now a showplace. We were conducted through the palace and our lecturer described all we saw to us as we went along.

The Royal Chapel has a floor, which is all mosaic. This will convey a faint idea of the splendour of its interior decorations and finish. The historical and biblical paintings on the ceilings and walls of the interior were very beautiful to me and are no doubt works of art. We walked through the bedroom of the unfortunate Louis and saw his bed. Much of the original furniture is still in the castle, although a large quantity was pillaged and destroyed in the troubled times. Looking into the grounds, one can visualize the howling bloodthirsty hordes that surrounded the castle in 1791, bent on the destruction of the French monarchy, which ended on that day. We were in the room where the peace treaty between the Germans and the Allies was signed in 1919 and saw the table on which the document was placed. We were shown Queen Marie Antoinette's bedroom and boudoirs – also some of the old tapestries. The wood carving, brass work and mural and other decorations are very interesting. Saw the Royal chariots which are used on state occasions. Had lunch at a nice restaurant near the palace. After

NO NEED TO WEAR RUBBERS

which we walked a short distance to the Petit Trianon, a small palace which King Louis had erected for the Queen and where Marie Antoinette hid herself when she needed a rest from court functions and routine.

Versailles is a beautifully appointed castle and one cannot but think of the feelings of the unhappy queen, dragged from this wonder house of comfort and splendour and pushed unceremoniously into a prison dungeon, there to languish for 10 weeks, uncared for and unattended, until she was beheaded on the guillotine, which put an end to her earthly existence.

Our next stop was at the interesting palace of Malmaison, where the Emperor Napoleon spent much time with his wife Josephine and which he had built especially for her. We saw Napoleon's bed and many other peaceful and warlike relics of him, including much of the golden dinner service used here. This also is now a national monument and, as such, is preserved. Returned to Paris at 6:00 p.m. After dinner I went for a walk and saw Paris on Sunday night. Such crowds! It was practically impossible to get through the streets. At 8:00 p.m. I started out to find the Casino de Paris to see a review, *Bonjour Paris!* in two acts and 45 tableaux.[11] I paid 31 francs for a ticket, one and a half francs to have my coat and hat checked, two francs for a programme which I could not read it, being in French, one franc to my usher and one franc for the hire of an opera glass. A total of about $1.90.

The performance was splendid. The costumes, dresses and stage settings were very elaborate, but I missed much through not understanding the French language. The 30 piece orchestra gave us plenty of good music. The actresses in one scene threw paper balls among the audience. This appeared to me to be a very interesting item, as there was much excitement. Those who succeeded in catching balls were awarded prizes which were delivered by chorus girls whose dresses were so abridged as to be almost non-

TRAVEL DIARY OF JAMES O'NEIL

This elegant cover, for the Paris Opera's 1925 season at the Académie Nationale de Musique et de Danse, cost my father two francs. He took great pleasure in attending the three-part matinée on March 11, 1925. Unfortunately he only had time to attend one performance, but it starred two of the leading French classical artists. (Académie Nationale de Musique et de Danse)

existent. In the last scene, the performers, who crowded the stage in all directions, threw more paper balls among the audience, who threw them back, and for a while things were lively. I grabbed and threw back one ball, but did not register a bull's eye. Flowers were also thrown quite freely. We were out at midnight and after a short walk, I went to the hotel and to bed.

March 9 (Monday)

Cold and fine. Left with Cook's at 10:30 a.m. Did a second tour of the city, did this with the afternoon excursion on Saturday. It practically completes a circuit of the most interesting parts of Paris. Saw the Tuileries Gardens and buildings, Chamber of Deputées, Palace de L'Élysée (official residence of the president), also the Arc de Triomphe, built by Napoleon to celebrate his victories. This immense stone arch stands 180 feet high. Beneath the center of the arch is the grave of the unknown soldier, with a fire continually burning over it and roped off by a chain.

In the distance I saw the Eiffel Tower, which is about 1,000 feet high, designed by Alexandre Gustave Eiffel a French Engineer, who designed and erected the tower for the Paris Exhibition of 1889. The Trocadéro is a state owned theatre and, like the Eiffel Tower, was built to commemorate the previous French Exhibition in 1878.

The admission fee here is very low and all artists who come to Paris – singers, actors, actresses, musicians, or whoever they may be, or however high their class – are compelled to come and perform at the Trocadéro for the benefit of those who cannot pay the high prices demanded at the regular theatres. This is a municipal ordinance and brings the world's greatest artists within the line of vision of the humble and poorer classes. We next visited Napoleon's tomb, where the Emperor lies buried.

The electric street signs are very good, but not to be compared with New York's. One may sit out in chairs on the sidewalks and have drinks or refreshments served under an awning or arcade, which is in front of almost all cafés. In some of those street café extensions, there are stoves on the sidewalk to heat up the patrons. I went to the famous Harry's New York Bar tonight. I saw his advertisement in the Paris edition of the *Daily Mail*. This paper is printed in Paris daily and is in English. It is an edition of the English *Daily Mail* published in London, England. Needless to say, this paper was welcome to me, as I was glad to see an English paper with a bit of late world news.

Harry kept a saloon in New York, USA, in pre-prohibition days and when the Volsted Act[12] came in force hied himself to pastures new, migrated to Paris and there opened a café and cabaret. His hope was to pick up English speaking travellers and judging from the number of patrons, I think that from a financial standpoint Harry's move was a good one. One would almost think on entering here that he was in New York. I met many English and American travellers and English was the predominant language spoken here. There was a cabaret from 10:00 p.m. to 2:00 a.m. and I really enjoyed the time. Quite a few of the girls, and there were many here, spoke English.

I found Harry's place by asking at the hotel how far it was. Then, I wrote the name and address on a slip of paper, which I kept showing to the police, who pointed me the direction, until I ultimately found Harry's. Immorality is rampant in Paris. Hotels are provided for lustful purposes. One is continually being held up on the street by girls, by men vendors of filthy pictures, also by men who offer to act as your guide and take you to see a special show, as they call it. These shows are the lowest forms of human depravity.

NO NEED TO WEAR RUBBERS

March 10 (Tuesday)

In the forenoon, I went by elevator to the top of the Eiffel Tower. This is an all steel structure and partly owing to its great height was the most powerful wireless station in the world during the Great War. There are four floors, on the first of which is a theatre, restaurant, café, souvenir counter, photo studio, etc. The second floor is about the same as the first, but not quite so large. The elevator stops at every floor and one may get off at any floor and wait for the next elevator, which will be along in 10 minutes. The trip to the top costs five francs.

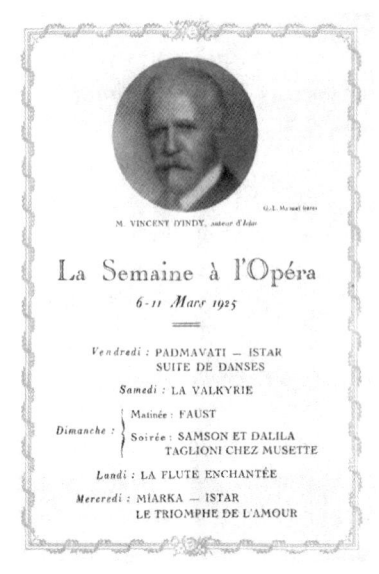

Beneath this photo of the acclaimed composer, Vincent d'Indy, is the program for the week of March 6 - 11, 1925 at the Opera. It includes information about Wednesday's three one-act offerings Miarka, Istar, *and* Le Triomphe De L'Amour. *(Académie Nationale de Musique et de Danse)*

I treated myself to a cognac and light lunch 1,000 feet above the city. The view from here is a very fine one. I was fortunate in being favoured with a fine day. There are two large, well kept parks on two sides of the tower; in fact, it may be said to be built in a park. The city and surroundings roll on for miles in all directions. As far as we can see from this lofty eminence, there appears no end to Paris and its environs. The wide and extensive boulevards and open spaces to be seen from here are quite refreshing in comparison with the congestion of the average city.

I passed through a section of the city where many buildings are being erected for the art exhibition which is to open May 1. Those buildings cover quite a large section. One bridge over the river, closed to traffic, is also being used for those miniature structures which represent modern and ancient art. In the afternoon, I visited many points of interest and at night, went to a show at the Palace Theatre at 27 francs, three francs for a programme and one for the usher. An enjoyable variety performance. The lighting effects in the scenes were well conducted. The fountain scene and orange groves of California were very real productions. Maurice Chevalier is the leading man here. He is a good actor and appears to be quite a popular idol with the audience. Yvonne Vallée is the very capable leading lady. Although I enjoyed the show from start to finish, still as in other performances, which I have witnessed in this country and Spain, I missed much of the merit through not being familiar with the language of the players.

After leaving the show about midnight, I was slowly wending my way toward my hotel when I was passed by a rather big man who

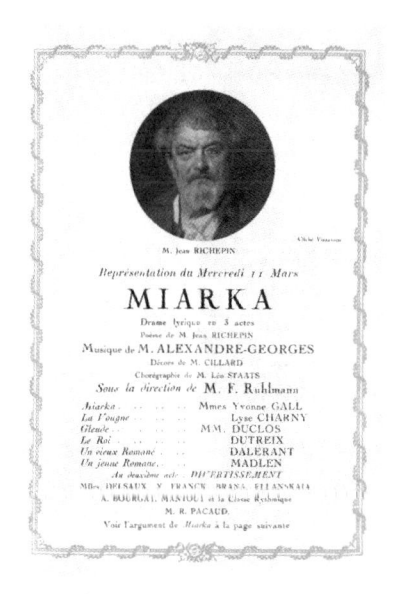

A page from the Académie program for Wednesday, March 11, 1925, relates to Miarka, *a lyric drama in three scenes, based on a poem by Jean Richepin, with music by M. Alexandre-Georges. Lyric dramas were musical or operatic songs which expressed the poet's feelings rather than telling of outward incidents or events. (Académie Nationale de Musique et de Danse)*

Considered as one of the most beautiful, as well as most popular French opera singers of her day, the diva Yvonne Gall starred in the Drame Lyrique, Miarka, *in three scenes.* (Académie Nationale de Musique et de Danse)

was going in my direction and who was under the influence of liquor (rather an unusual sight in France). He jostled me, and said in English (more to himself than to me), "I'm as drunk as Hell." I was glad to hear the English language and took a chance, after some preliminaries, in picking up an acquaintance. This man, who was equally glad to meet one speaking the language, turned out to be a lumber dealer from Canada and he insisted on my coming to a hotel for supper with him. We went to Rose's for supper. Had a swell meal, washed down by copious draughts of champagne and about 2:00 a.m. I went with him in a taxi to his hotel, the Continental, and from there to my hotel and bed.

March 11 (Wednesday)

Wet snow falling. Paris has many narrow streets, as well as wide and beautiful boulevards. Bought my ticket today at Cook's for an aeroplane flight to London. I am to leave the Grand Hotel tomorrow at 10:30 a.m. in a bus for the aerodrome at Le Bourget. In the afternoon, I went to a movie. The picture was of an ill-fated expedition to Mount Everest. Eight or ten Tibetans (some of whom had accompanied the expedition) were present, acting in the capacity of an orchestra. They played very strange instruments and their music and singing was most unusual and to me most doleful. This show cost 12 francs, two for a programme, and one for the usher.

At night I attended an opera, *Miarka*,[13] by Alexandre-Georges at the Paris Opera House – Académie Nationale de Musique et de Danse. My seat cost 35 francs. Evening dress for men is compulsory in many sections of the theatre and it is a fundamental rule that no patron is admitted unless he is dressed in a very dark suit. I secured a very good seat. This is the most wonderful theatre I have seen to date. There were four floors of boxes all round the theatre. The interior finish is marvellous. The opera was good and the singing, to those who appreciated or understood it, was no doubt of a very high order. During the first intermission, of which there were three, about two-thirds of the audience left their seats and went outside. I, thinking the interval would be short, remained in my seat and was surprised to find this intermission fully a half-hour long.

At the start of the second interval, I followed the crowd and was well rewarded, as

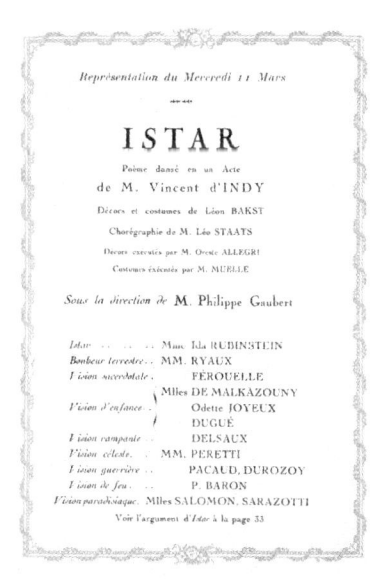

The Académie program for March 11, 1925 lists the cast of Istar, *a dance poem performed in one act, to the music of Vincent D'Indy. Born in Paris in 1851 to a family of the ancient nobility and a pupil of César Franck, he became one of the great French composers.* Istar *was written as symphonic variations for orchestra in 1896.* (Académie Nationale de Musique et de Danse)

NO NEED TO WEAR RUBBERS

Mme Ida RUBINSTEIN, interprète d'« Istar »

As a boy, I recall my father telling me, in his own humourous way, during one of the many times we were looking at his Académie programme, that the acclaimed Russian ballerina, Ida Rubenstein, whom he saw dance the role of Istar, *never had a waist as thin as that depicted on this page, because she would not have been able to eat. Born in Russia and a leading dancer with the Mariinsky Theatre (later known as the Kirov Ballet) in St. Petersburg, Rubenstein had a hugely successful career when she came to the west.* (Académie Nationale de Musique et de Danse)

The largest theatre in Paris in 1925 was Le Palais du Trocadéro. It had seating accommodation for almost 8,000 people. Built in 1878 for the Paris Exhibition, the Palais survived until 1937, when it was replaced by the current Palais de Chaillot as a location for the Exposition of the Arts. (N.D. Photo)

I saw many things that interested me more than the singing of operatic stars. The Opera House is a massive and extensive building from the outside, whereas the theatre is comparatively small. On entering the lobby from the main floor, I found myself in the company of crowds of the most gaily dressed women I have ever seen, as well as smart looking, immaculately groomed men. All were promenading leisurely around the beautiful and artistic galleries, which are immense and run in all directions.

There were tiers of balconies in the lobby, three or four in height. In those, men and women lounged, sipped their champagne and smoked or stood prominently forward, as if to exhibit their physical, as well as artistic, beauty. There were many bars selling liquors and, as I sipped my wine at 1:00 a.m., I thought to myself well perhaps the man at the next table may be Clemenceau,[14] Briand[15] or some other world famed Frenchman, as I felt (and not without a slight thrill of

NO NEED TO WEAR RUBBERS

In this view of la Place de L'Opéra, we see the magnificent Paris Opera house, which was home to the Académie Nationale de Musique et de Danse of which my father writes in some detail regarding a performance he saw there in 1925. (N.D. Photo)

pride) that I was hobnobbing with France's aristocracy.

This intermission with its frills appeared to me to be of more importance to the gathering than the opera. I sat off for 10 minutes or more in a big overstuffed chair and saw a stream of the most stylishly dressed and bejewelled women it has ever been my privilege to behold. People just sat and stared at this endless procession and this staring appeared to be quite in order. One would almost think himself in the stock exchange, there was so much talk and gesticulating; but alas yours truly had no one to whom he could unburden his wondering soul, as he was a lone stranger in a strange land. I enjoyed the ever-changing scene, smoked and strutted round rubbing elbows with the possessors of the most elaborately and completely groomed whiskers, as well as corpulent, underdressed specimens of femininity, and felt quite at home. When the gong sounded to come back to the theatre for the next act, I realized, for the first time since leaving Newfoundland, I was absolutely lost. First, I did not know in which direction the theatre lay and second, I would not know where my entrance was, even if I could locate the theatre. I was worried about my hat and coat, which had been checked in at the cloakroom situated at the entrance I came in through. I could not, of course, ask questions because, "Je ne parle pas français."

After some time I espied a very conspicuous figure, a large, happy looking man who had been seated just a short distance in front of me and filled his theatre seat to over-flowing, and had attracted

The Panthéon de la Guerre, formerly a Roman Catholic church, at the end of Rue Soufflot, is now a national monument and museum. In 1925 the Panthéon, a circular building, contained a wonderful painting on a canvas 450 feet long and 42 feet high, which is described in the diary. (N.D. Photo)

The Eiffel Tower has become the symbol of France throughout the world, sharing its fame as an international landmark with the Statue of Liberty, a gift from France to the United States of America. This photo, from 1925, is remarkable for its lack of traffic on the road running beside the bank of the river Seine. (N.D. Photo)

my attention by standing in that seat several times during the performance, while looking in all directions through his opera glasses. To me the benevolent gent appeared to be a sheik, but whatever he was, he was my good angel as I kept close in his wake until he landed in his little used set, which also brought me to mine. No smoking is allowed in the theatre of the opera house. One may hire a pair of opera glasses by dropping a coin in slot machines on the backs of the chairs. It was quite common during the performance to see several men standing in different parts of the theatre at the same time, looking round, with and without opera glasses. Whether they stood to look or to be looked at, I could not get clear in my mind. Some ladies of the audience, in the boxes, stood up prominently at times, which was a signal for a barrage of glasses to be immediately turned on the spot where the latest resurrection had taken place. Many men wore opera hats. These are shaped like a beaver hat, but are of silk and collapsible. When collapsed they are usually placed on the seat and sat on. I won't soon forget the surprise I got when I first saw a man place his hat on a chair and sit on it. Had I been sufficiently near him, I probably would have told him that he was sitting on his hat as, needless to say, a collapsible hat was an innovation to me. My thoughts during the opera and intermissions were pleasantly varied.

The performance finished about midnight and then came the jam of motor cars, which took the patrons to their homes or night clubs. I arrived at my hotel at 1:30 a.m. The public toilets on the streets amuse me, as it appears that privacy is non-essential. On almost every block of the streets at night, the foreigner (and I may add the stranger is known here) is held up by the question: "Do you want a guide, sir?" or "Want to see the special show, sir?" You have just rounded the bows of the would-be guide, when you find yourself almost in collision with a wee scrap of feminine humanity, painted, powdered and trim, saying "Weel you cam weeth me, meester? Me nice gal. Speck Anglay." You show that you are not interested and immediately comes the plaintive "Porquoi (her English is now exhausted), meester?"

One thing particularly I missed in Paris was the sight of the deep blue sea, so dear to the heart of a Newfoundlander.

LONDON

March 12 (Thursday)

Changed 200 francs to English money at Cook's and received two pounds, three shillings. When I had paid my hotel bill (which I tried to do quietly), I found myself surrounded by waiter, lift

This view of Big Ben, at the north end of London Bridge, shows the Parliament tower of Westminster Palace. The name is given to a bell in the tower and also to a huge tower clock. The Palace on the right houses the British Parliament. (Doug Lynch)

man, chamber maid, head porter, etc., etc., all waiting for the tip. This tip might be amusing if it were not so expensive. I then taxied to the Grand Hotel, for which I paid the rather insignificant sum of five francs, with of course, a tip. On arrival, the porter took my grips inside the hotel – another tip. When the bus for the passengers going to the aerodrome arrived, and my grips were deposited on board – another tip. Ten passengers left at 11:30 a.m., and in about a half an hour we arrived at the French aerodrome of Le Bourget.

The following notes I took on my flight from Paris to London:

• *Left aerodrome in a two-engined, cabin aeroplane of the French Line with 10 passengers, one being a lady, also a pilot and mechanic, (total 12) at 12:43 p.m.*
• *It is very cold and snowing. Owing to snowstorm no planes crossed over to England yesterday. Passed a plane, Paris bound at 1:43 p.m.*
• *Snowing at 2:10 p.m., clear again at 2:15 p.m. The land over which we have been flying for some time is very much overflowed with water.*
• *At 2:22 p.m., extensive tracts covered with sand underneath us. It is very bumpy. Our ship is rolling and pitching considerably. The sensation is as if one were on the ocean in a small boat, in a rather choppy sea.*
• *At 2:25 p.m., now over the English Channel in thick snow squalls. Since leaving Le Bourget, the plane has twice turned back, but continued again on its westward course. Why we turned, I don't know, but it is very stormy and frosty and generally an all round bad day.*
• *At 2:30 p.m., we are in the midst of white fleecy clouds, with our visibility very limited.*
• *At 2:35 p.m., I can now see the waters of the Channel. We are flying very high and above the clouds.*
• *At 2:45 p.m., we are still following the French Coast. It must be because of the snow. Since getting to this high altitude, above the clouds, the plane is very steady; no bumping.*

- At 2:47 p.m., nothing in sight except the sea, now and again, through the clouds. The sun is shining splendidly.
- At 2:55 p.m., we are still sailing along smoothly, above the clouds. There is just a slight vibration in the plane. One would think it stopped, so steady are we gliding along, but this would not be a particularly happy place to stop. I am now getting accustomed to the noise from the propellers. It is very cold and the passengers are doing all possible to keep warm. Just now we passed through a cloud and got a bit of a bump.
- At 3:10 p.m., no land in sight. Our one lady passenger is refreshing herself with sandwiches and appears quite content and happy. Personally, I'd like a hot scotch just now.
- At 3:17 p.m., through a rift in the clouds below, I can see the coast of Merrie England. The feeling I have up here is of absolute security.
- At 3:25 p.m., we are nearing the coast. Steamers are in sight, but they look quite small.
- At 3:28 p.m., two steamers are almost directly under us. I can see the foam from them. It is blowing half a gale from the N. East.
- At 3:30 p.m., we are now straight over the English Coast. The houses look very small.
- At 3:35 p.m., passing over what looks like an agricultural district. Occasional glimpses of the ground are seen through the clouds.
- At 3:38 p.m., farms look beautiful, but the homes and other buildings are so tiny. Can now see the roads as the merest strips of white.
- At 3:50 p.m., we are now flying lower, as I can see motor cars moving on the roads.
- At 3:56 p.m., passing over a town.
- At 4:02 p.m., can now see pedestrians in the roads. Beautiful farms, estates and forests almost the whole way from the coast.
- At 4:05 p.m., passing over a village or small town. We are surely coming nearer to mother earth, as the objects below are growing. It is bumpy again down here (bumping is caused by small air pockets or wind eddies and is not at all dangerous). Apparently the road has not been repaired on this level. Our lady friend is now powdering her nose, I suppose in anticipation of landing very soon.

TRAVEL DIARY OF JAMES O'NEIL

London's Westminster Abbey is a national shrine and the scene of coronations of all English monarchs since William I. The name comes from the fact that the church of a Benedictine Abbey once stood here. Inside is the burial place of kings, queens and distinguished British subjects. (Doug Lynch)

• At 4:12 p.m., the engines are running perceptibly slower, so we must be near our landing place.
• At 4:13 p.m., we are circling over Croydon Field, London. I can see the name Croydon in large white letters on the grass.
• At 4:14 p.m., landed beautifully and taxied in the plane up to the aerodrome.

On arrival, the pilot told us we had crossed at an altitude of 6,300 feet.

He was forced to go up there on account of the snow, but he said he was fearful that his radiators may freeze, as they were not fitted to contend with severe frost, like today's. On fine days, they cross the channel at about 3,500 feet altitude.

The noise in the plane was not so bad. Over every seat there was a fixture, with a supply of cotton wool, to plug ones ears. Passengers, who sat in individual seats, were supplied with a heavy rug and cushions under and over the foot. We talked a little coming over and moved round the car. Luggage was free up to 30 pounds, or 12 kilos. Over that amount, the charge was one and a half francs a kilo. The passage over cost 400 francs. By rail and steamer, I could have got from Paris to London for about 250 francs.

On the plane's arrival at Croydon, two, five-passenger motor cars are waiting to take the new arrivals to their homes or hotels in London. This, as well as the bus ride to the aerodrome in Paris, is paid for in the ticket. Croydon is 210 miles from Le Bourget, as the crow flies. The route in good weather is 245 miles. The average time is two and a half hours. The fastest time for a large machine is one hour and fifty-minutes. We were (due to bad weather) three and a half hours in the air.

I came over on the French airline. There is also an English line using Handley Page engines. On arrival, we met the customs men who examined our baggage and passports. They did not even look in our grips, which I suppose was through consideration, as we were a hungry and cold looking bunch. After about 15 minutes, we left and in a short time I was housed at the Imperial Hotel, Russell Square, with room and breakfast (no bath) for 10 pounds and six shillings.

After a wash, I had a hot drink, then back to dinner which cost five shillings, six pence for a tip, 10 pence for a bottle of Bass, and six pence to the bell hop for my hat and coat. Bought a guide book and map of London at the hotel, which is a fairly large one and in which there is a Thomas Cook and Son's Office. At 8:00 p.m., went to a movie or, as they call it here, a cinema show. Saw Jackie Coogan in *Young Robinson Crusoe*. After the show, went for a walk and met several lassies who, from their broad smiles in my direction and winsome, pleased expressions, appeared very happy that I had arrived at the great metropolis. These females are not as aggressive and persistent as the Paris mademoiselles. I have since learnt that the law is more strict here on those girls than in Paris. Back to the hotel about midnight.

After hobnobbing with Spaniards and French for nearly a month, I looked forward, with some pleasurable anticipation, to the day when I would arrive in England where I could understand the language. But, I am forced to admit, I have not understood one word of every 10 I heard spoken since I landed here, and few understand me unless I repeat myself once or twice.

March 13 (Friday)

Had a good breakfast. This is the first real, honest to goodness breakfast I have had since leaving the S.S. *Agga* at Alicante. It consisted of cereal, fish, ham and eggs, toast, rolls, coffee and marmalade. After a short walk, I took a taxi, and drove to Harrington & White's Office, Leadenhall Street, and called on Arthur Bremner,[16] and incidently collected 12 shillings and 6 pence, a balance which was to the credit of my account at this office for about two years. Bremner and I went out, took a seat on top of a bus and I saw a bit of London. Nearly all double-deck motor buses used here. Surface street cars are not much in evidence. Lunched at the British Empire Club and was given a complimentary ticket enti-

NO NEED TO WEAR RUBBERS

tling me to the use of the club for a month. After lunch, walked across the Thames. It is a noble river. Passed Buckingham Palace.

At Cook's office I bought a ticket for an all-day tour of London tomorrow, which cost 25 shillings; also I bought a ticket for tonight for the Criterion Theatre, the performance being a play entitled *Just Married* [a 1921 New York and London hit]. Ticket cost nine pounds, six shillings. Took a bus to Piccadilly, where I spent a half hour, then another bus to the hotel. At 8:00 p.m. I left for the theatre. It was raining and I, not knowing the direction, took a taxi. Taxi charges here are one shilling for the first ten minutes. It was probably a ten minute ride from the theatre, but it took me about 25 minutes to get there, as there was a heavy traffic jam and we were held up many times. The taxi trip cost two pounds, six shillings, and on arrival at the destination I had to go underground to the theatre. I rather unwillingly parted with my coat and hat at the cloakroom, for which I paid sixpence.

The play was a comedy. Lynn Overman, the leading man is an excellent actor. The play ended, I went for my hat and coat, but evidently I went the wrong way. I tried to get back, but it was no use as I was taken, jostled, and carried along with the crowd until I lost all sense of direction. I thought I went up sufficient stairs to be at the top of a building of ordinary height before I got free from the jam. After getting clear, I raced down halls and stairs, until I eventually found the cloakroom, and to my great relief I redeemed my coat and hat. The section where this theatre is situated is wonderfully well-lit by electric signs and, as I enjoyed a half hour's walk through the gay throngs, I was strongly reminded of Broadway. Home by taxi, having greatly enjoyed my first full day in London. I find things more expensive here than in Spain or France.

TRAVEL DIARY OF JAMES O'NEIL

My father mentions passing Queen Alexandra's home in London, which is today Marlborough House. He also writes of the Horse Guard's Parade. This photo, taken over half a century ago, shows one of the Horse Guards standing at the entrance to the Parade grounds. (Doug Lynch)

NO NEED TO WEAR RUBBERS

March 14 (Saturday)

Went on a Cook's Tour. Saw much of London. Visited the historical Tower of London where we saw large collection of armour, old weapons, Lord Kitchener's Sword, the Crown Jewels, gold dinner service, etc. This was once the palace of the kings, later a famous or infamous prison and now is a barracks for soldiers where about a 1,000 with their families are housed. It covers 12 acres. Among many other things, I saw the block and axe used in former days at executions, also the gibbet. I stood near the stone which marks the spot where Henry VIII's wife, Anne Boleyn, was beheaded. We were also shown inscriptions cut hundreds of years ago by prisoners on the walls of some of the cells, which are about three feet thick. The tower and its contents are guarded by a special detachment of troops in picturesque costumes of the Elizabethan age; they are known as Beefeaters.

Visited the great Church of England Cathedral of St. Paul's, and saw its beautiful dome. Nelson, Wellington, Lord Roberts,[17] and other notables are buried here. A crucifix hangs above the altar. From St. Paul's we went to Westminster Abbey, where many English monarchs are buried; the last monarch to be interred there being Elizabeth, whose tomb I saw. The unknown soldier is buried under the floor just inside the main entrance. Many poets are buried here; in fact a part of the edifice is called the poet's corner where Browning, Tennyson, etc., are buried. The Abbey is adorned by an immense amount of statuary of the Empire's great men. The monarchs of England are crowned here and I saw the coronation chair in which all English royalty have been crowned for 600 hundred years. The chair is rather dilapidated and is not much to look at, but it is, of course, a priceless antique. I saw nothing here to remind one of God, but some cardinal's hats, which hung from the ceiling, brought back memories of Catholic days.

Later we saw Queen Alexandra's home [Marlborough House, Pall Mall, where the Queen Mother lived until her death in 1925], and the famous Horse Guards Parade. Then went to Buckingham Palace opposite, which is the picturesque Albert Memorial. Visited the Strand, Marble Arch, Hyde Park and St. James' Park. Spent some time on a tour of the Parliament Buildings, where I walked through the Houses of Commons and Lords. Saw the king's robing room and his seat in the House of Lords, as well as those of the queen and princes. The legislative chambers are rather small and to me appeared somewhat stuffy, but the paintings, frescoes, mosaics, as well as other decorations and furnishings, were, to say the least, very interesting and the chambers were venerable to me.

Saw the prime minister's official seat, as well as the seats of other celebrities. Visited the chamber in the basement in which the late King Edward VII and Prime Minister Gladstone had lain in state previous to their burial. Paid a very interesting, but short visit, to the British Museum, where there is a most wonderful collection. Saw much old statuary there from the period BC. I met an Indian gentleman from Simla, India, on today's tour. He is working in the British Foreign Office there and was on a very extended holiday. He spoke English fluently, as he had been educated in England. He and I became quite friendly. His name was Staggs, or rather that was the name he was then using.

This was a nice warm day, but at night, it rained, which prevented me from getting out around. A dinner dance at the hotel this evening was a crowded and enjoyable affair. We had but six passengers on our Cook's tour in the morning, but filled up in the afternoon. Have spent some time studying my map of London, but have not got very far with it.

NO NEED TO WEAR RUBBERS

March 15 (Sunday)

After attending 9:00 a.m. mass, I left the Imperial Hotel at 10 pounds, six shillings and removed to the National Hotel at eight pounds, six shillings and no tips. This is the hotel where my Indian friend Staggs is staying. At 11:30 a.m., Staggs and I took an underground train to Hyde Park and spent some time there and at St. James Park. At 3:00 p.m., attended a concert in the Albert Hall at three pounds, six shillings and heard the world-famed pianist Rummel,[18] also an Italian singer of note, Mademoiselle Paikin, who sang in Italian, French and Russian.

After the concert, my friend and I went to dinner at the Cosmo Hotel, Bloomsbury Square, after which we went to Piccadilly, where we spent some time, then to Leicester Square and Charing Cross. During our saunter, we heard some soapbox orators at Hyde Park Corner, holding forth. One of them was raising Cain, criticising the British Government and British shipbuilding companies, because England failed to get the contract to build the *Caribou* for Newfoundland. There were large crowds on the street and some drunkenness was in evidence. Saw an old woman gloriously drunk and two pals of hers about half-seas-over, with their bonnets tilted at a dangerous angle, presumably taking her home.

March 16 (Monday)

To London Museum with Staggs and spent the forenoon there. Saw many of Queen Victoria's dresses, her coronation robes, innumerable antiques, the remains of a large Roman galley and a prison cell complete from Old Newgate Prison, with inscriptions cut in the stone walls by prisoners. Saw many instruments of torture used in the old days. After lunch, I took a bus for Camden Town and from there I went alone to the zoo. This compares very favourably with the zoo at the Bronx Park, New York. There is certainly a very interesting collection of animals, birds, reptiles, etc. Here, in fact, one may see almost everything that is alive on the land today, from the lordly elephant or camel, to the insignificant mosquito.

I visited the Aquarium, which is the home of the fishes. This also was of great interest to me, as the diversity of fish was very great and they all appeared quite happy; each species in its own particular environment. To see the fishes swimming in their little cells, with glass fronts, formed pretty pictures. Left at 5:00 p.m., after a most enjoyable afternoon and with some difficulty found Camden Station where I took a bus to Russell Square, which was quite near where my hotel was located. At night saw a musical comedy, *No, No, Nannette*,[19] which was good. My ticket cost five pounds, nine shillings and six pence for programme and usher. To get to the theatre, I went by underground railway from Russell Square to Leicester Square.

Since noon today, this is the first time I have been on my own hook in London and I have done fairly well. I have now got confidence enough to think I can get around. The underground trains are very simple. Maps and other guiding marks make travelling for the stranger quite easy. Lifts or elevators, holding about 50, take passengers from the street level down to the underground trains. My judgement is that the average drop from the street to the level on which the underground trains run is about 50 or 60 feet. The trains are long and very swift. Took the underground from Leicester Square to Russell Square after the show. On arrival at Russell Square Station, lifts take passengers up to the street level. Staggs is at a dance tonight.

NO NEED TO WEAR RUBBERS

Trafalgar Square, named for Lord Nelson's victory over the French in the Battle of Trafalgar, is the site of Nelson's Pillar in the heart of London where crowds throng amidst pigeons and fountain spray. The death of Nelson, as depicted at the base of the column, is by Irish sculptor John Edward Carew who created the statues of St. Patrick, St. Francis and St. John the Baptist in the Roman Catholic Basilica, St. John's, Newfoundland. In the background (left) is the famous church of St. Martin's in the Fields. On the right is South Africa House. (Paul O'Neill)

March 17 (Tuesday)

After attending mass at Holburn at 10:00 a.m., I went to Buckingham Palace to see the changing of the guard. This is quite impressive and is a daily occurrence, which takes place with quite a bit of ceremony. The guard's band, of upwards of 50 or more instruments, accompanied the guard for the day to the palace. They stand in the grounds playing beautifully while the guard is being changed and later accompany the relieved guard back to barracks. The guard is comprised of a goodly number of soldiers who are composed of the English, Irish and Scots Grenadier Guards. They are the flower of the British Army and, I might add, with their grey great coats, rolled blankets on backs, immaculately white belts and blanket straps, topped by a high black fur cap, they looked like stunning specimens of humanity.

As King George V is indisposed, the soldiers left the grounds with a slow step, with the band silent. After getting some distance from the gates, the band struck up a lively quick march. I saw footmen at the palace door in their scarlet satin costumes with breeches. From the palace walked to Alexandra House, home of the Queen Mother. I passed by the residence of the Prince of Wales and continued on to Westminster Roman Catholic Cathedral. The interior of this church is not yet fully completed. Some of the chapels, however, are finished in mosaics and coloured marble, etc. Massive white and gold marble columns are everywhere to be seen and its pulpit, which is completed, struck me very forcibly and is the last word in mosaics. Cardinal Vaughan was the founder. He died in 1903, its opening year. It is 360 feet long by 156 feet wide and in its construction 12.5 million bricks were used. Cardinal Vaughan's body is buried in a Cathedral chapel dedicated to him, known as the Vaughan chapel. There is a recumbent effigy of him on his tomb. This vast modern church [in the Byzantine style of the Eastern Roman Empire] is in a congested area, which undoubtedly mars its beauty, if it has any architectural beauty, which is a very debatable question. Many English critics as well as those of other countries are divided in their opinions on this point. The crypt, which I visited, contains the tombs of Cardinals Manning and Wiseman, the first bishops of Westminster. They are buried under the high altar of the cathedral and in the chapel of St. Edmunds, whose relic – a bone of his leg – is in plain view under the altar. There is also a Russian Ambassador (under the Czars) buried here. The tomb of Cardinal Manning is finished in Russian mosaic.

My next visit was Madam Tussaud's world famed wax works and chamber of horrors, etc. Soldiers, sailors and police in wax, but looking very real and life-like, guard the entrance. I might add I did not know they were wax. There are life-size and very life-like images of the great men and women of the world. We find kings, queens, soldiers, poets, boxers; in fact, men and women in all walks of life who for some reason have become famous or notorious. All are there in their respective uniforms, regalia or dress. Some of the latter are very elaborate as well as very quaint, such as soldiers in full dress with their swords, medals and decorations. I was rather struck with Kitchener, Haig and Foch. From their prominence in the world war and, having seen so many pictures of them in recent years, they appeared quite familiar.

Mary Queen of Scots may be seen standing there. Above her, with outstretched hand, and in an attitude of blessing or preaching, is Martin Luther. I thought the placing rather inappropriate. Every figure was numbered and a guide book costing sixpence, gave all the information needed. Saw Henry VIII in armour surrounded by his six wives. From appearances, I thought Daniel O'Connell [20] and Martin Luther were two outstanding figures among the celebrities. One needed to look twice at visitors who were standing still, to be sure they were not wax figures.

One large square was reserved for present day English Royalty. In it were King George, Queen Mary, the Prince of Wales and Princess Mary, with the King of Spain and some others. All were in elaborate uniforms or magnificent dresses. An orchestra was playing. Rooms off the wax works were given over to Napoleon. Here were the state carriages and his coronation robes, as well as his garden chair and camp equipage from St. Helena. There were many pictures and other interesting objects.

From the Napoleon rooms, I went down the stairs to the Chamber

TRAVEL DIARY OF JAMES O'NEIL

of Horrors and had a creepy feeling up my back as I reached the bottom. I was standing among scores of the greatest criminals and most bloodthirsty murderers the world has known. Some of those criminals, or rather their replicas in wax, were well-dressed, well-groomed and fair of face, whereas others were repugnant and brutal looking. Here was the English pillory of former days and the French guillotine, along with ropes, with their spliced loops, that had been used at the hangings of many victims, hung on the wall. There were horrible instruments of torture from Old Newgate, other prisons and elsewhere, with many devices of chains and irons used for manacling prisoners strewn round. I was in the prison cell in which Lord George Gordon[21] (who is a prominent personage in Dickens' *Barnaby Rudge*) died. This cell was removed intact from Old Newgate Prison. It contained a crude bunk built against the wall, a heavy deal table and a chain. The old toll bell from the same prison is here. The inscription on the bell reads:

"Ye people all who hear me ring, Be faithful to your God and King."

Many scenes were staged in the Hall of Tableau, which adjoins the Chamber of Horrors. There was included the execution of Mary Queen of Scots, the Death of Nelson in his Cabin on board HMS *Victory*, the Martyrdom of Thomas Becket in Canterbury Cathedral, December 29, 1170 as well as many other such displays.

I have just given a few of the horrible and interesting things to be seen here. I spent three or four hours and at 4:00 p.m., went to Leadenhall Street again to see Mr. Bremner. Have noticed today, as on former occasions, many small steam engines, miniature locomotives pulling coal trucks about the streets. In fact, it looks to me as if all the coal is delivered here in this way. Back to the hotel via Piccadilly and to the Cosmo to dinner. Had a walk and noted that the taxi and other drivers are very much in awe of the police, also that the police are very polite and take great pains and show considerable patience in directing the strangers. No Patrick's Day celebrations greeted me today.

March 18 (Wednesday)

Spent the forenoon in the Natural Histories Museum. Saw some Newfoundland stuffed seals and birds there, also some enormous seals from the South Seas. Saw many precious stones, stuffed animals and birds. There is one large room given to minerals. Many things pertaining to the study of natural history are here. It would take a week to see all the exhibits. There are innumerable examples of the Stone Age, as well as all other ages of history, and all amazingly in good order.

Left at noon and went to Leadenhall Street and, being joined by Bremner who now took upon himself the duty of guide, we went off together and after driving through some extremely narrow streets and alleys, for which the city of London is renowned, we eventually stood at the bar of a liquor saloon, or club, which is perhaps the correct term, which seemed as if it was burrowed in the earth. I noted we were in a very busy place and that many of the patrons were attired in their silk or beaver hats, Prince Albert coats and, of course, the inseparable umbrella. Those were businessmen from the Bank and Leadenhall Street district. After we had partaken of a glass of scotch, which undoubtedly was the drawing card for the assembled crowd, we left for pastures new and after making several turns and walking through further narrow streets, we finally anchored in what I may almost call a cellar for lunch.

This chop-house [a cheap, pub-like restaurant] is hundreds of years old and one must know something of the English character to realize how much they adhere to, love and admire the antique in all things pertaining to the nation. Apparently this is a popular resort, as it was packed with well-dressed men, who one could easily discern were businessmen, who had dropped in for lunch. I was told that in this part of the city, there were upwards of 1,000 of these small restaurants, many of them hundreds of years old, and still doing a thriving business. Among them is the one in which Charles Dickens took his lunch. This one is conducted today in the same way and with the same furnishings as when Dickens was a customer.

After lunch, we made another short trip and stopped at Ye Olde Inne, where we partook of coffee and port. The people here are fond of their whiskey and, in that, are a great contrast to the Frenchmen and Spaniards, who drink light wines and beers almost exclusively.

I have seen a few good jags since coming to London, particularly on Sunday night. The liquor laws are rather strange. Different parts of the city have different opening and closing hours. In my short stay, I could not understand them. Went to a new Bond Street tailor and ordered a suit of clothes, after which I took the underground to Brompton Road to see Harrods Stores. They occupy a whole block, about as long as Ayre's and Knowling's combined and on all four sides of the block, which means the stores are in four streets. They have a wonderfully select stock, but it is very high class. Queen Mary does most of her shopping here.[22]

There is a footman in a green brass buttoned greatcoat and cap in front of every entrance, to assist customers to and from their autos. The windows of Harrods, on the four sides, were very artistically dressed and the store was well worth a visit. After purchasing a silk handkerchief, I left, and just off Brompton Road saw street dancers, two elaborately painted and bangled girls and two men performing. Visited a Woolworth store, where no article is sold for more than six pence. I bought two pairs of socks for six pence a pair, as I thought, and which appeared to me, to be extra good value, but when I paid for them I found the price was six pence a sock. The store was very crowded with customers and it struck me that much goods must be stolen here, as the counters are piled high with socks. I also visited a poultry market where I saw turkey advertised for one pound, six shillings per pound. I did some necessary shopping this evening, as I do not anticipate spending much more time in London.

I arrived at Alicante on February 20 in the morning. It is now 27 days since I left the ship and my average daily expenditure (apart from any goods I have bought) is 10 dollars and 10 cents.

March 19 (Thursday)

Went in forenoon to see numbers 10 and 11 Downing Street. Those numbers represent the official residences of the English Prime Minister and his Minister of Finance, or chancellor, and few who visit London do not go to this street to see those historic old homes. They are gabled roofed, brick buildings and are very dingy, almost forbidding in appearance. The love of the antique, however, and the historical halo, which over hangs 10 and 11 Downing Street, will neither permit their being modernized, nor that the prime minister's residence be located in a more pretentious house and in a more select residential district. Downing Street is a very short street. It has a worldwide reputation and numbers 10 and 11 are the only residences. The Home Office with its smoke begrimed walls and its many blackened statues, which are set around its exterior walls, every few feet apart and about 20 feet from the ground, occupies the opposite side of the street.

I took a turn round the parliament buildings and heard Big Ben strike. Big Ben is a clock located in the tower of the parliament building. Again visited Westminster Abbey alone. My other visit here was with a Cook's Tour and I had very little time, but this old, world-renowned pile would well repay several visits, as it is one of the most interesting buildings, from a historical and religious standpoint, in England. On this visit I saw the tomb of Mary Queen of Scots, who was beheaded by orders of Queen Elizabeth; also the tomb of Edward the Confessor.

One tomb I saw here is 600 years old. Many of these older ones are disfigured. Many of the mosaics and other adornments were defaced or robbed during the many troubled periods. Some of the effigies are headless, that of Elizabeth having lost the crown and rose. The knights' chapel in the Abbey is a gem. The ceiling of it is carved stone, of a lace-work pattern, and the only one of its kind in existence. The interior walls of the Abbey are smoke tarnished, as this is a very smoky city; in fact a pall or blanket of smoke hovers over the city at all times, except on very fine days with a fairly good breeze of wind.

It is this smoke, combined with a foggy atmosphere, that creates the London fog, which the world has heard so much of and which is sometimes so thick, that all traffic is forced to stop. It turns day into black impenetrable darkness. Today it is fine, but one can scarcely see more than 30 feet through the smoky atmosphere. Walked across the Thames River and after several twistings and turnings, I found myself in filthy lanes and alleys. This undoubtedly was part of the London slums. Much squalor and poverty was in evidence and for more than an hour I walked through narrow streets, the condition of whose aimless looking adults and dirty, ragged and undernourished children would almost preclude the thought that I was in one of the greatest and wealthiest cities in the world.

It's a long road that has no turn, so after some considerable trouble I again found the bank of the river and re-crossed on another bridge, quite near the Tower of London. At one end of this bridge was a construction gang doing repair work and I stood for some time, an interested spectator, watching four men with hammers striking the same drill. I had seen two strikers at home striking one drill, but this was my first time to see four. I do not know if this is usual or not, but to me it appeared as if those strikers were very proficient. There was a constant rain of blows on the steel and never a miss.

I walked along Lower Thames Street and visited a large fresh fish market near the customs house. The smell of the fish, as well as the slub and oil clothes, were quite familiar. With very few of the varieties of fish seen here had I even a bowing acquaintance. Did some shopping and among others visited Selfridges general stores.[23] I had been tipped to visit here, as the store was celebrating its sixteenth birthday. The trimmed windows were visions of beauty. Some of them consisted of draped figures, stucco statues, artistic designs in landscape, fountains, flower beds, etc.

The street fronts were lavishly decorated with numerous pots of real flowers, ferns and creepers; also coloured festooning and bunting. The interior was illuminated with thousands of small electric bulbs, strung in all directions, on lines festooned with silver and gold leaves. Stucco figures were on pedestals and the general decorative effect brought to one's mind visions of fairyland. Outside the doors were the footmen, and inside were young girls dressed as pages who presented all who entered with a plan of the store, so that one had a minimum of trouble in locating any deserved department.

But oh, the crowds! I followed the line of least resistance and went whither I was carried in the jam. I was walked on, pushed, jostled and squeezed by women, as I found out after a while that I had unfortunately and unthinkingly got in the ladies' wear department. After a brief stay, I was unceremoniously – and perspiring in every pore – carried with the mob to the street. Having re-

TRAVEL DIARY OF JAMES O'NEIL

In the centre of Piccadilly Circus stands a fountain topped by a statue of Eros, the god of love. The fountain is a popular meeting place in West London. A famous street of shops, hotels, clubs, etc., extends from Piccadilly Circus to Hyde Park Corner. Half a block away is Leicester Square and the theatre district of Soho. (Paul O'Neill)

freshed myself with a bottle of Bass, I invaded the men's department. The rush here was about the same, but not being among the gentler sex now, I also could push and jostle and I made better headway. Several times I got jammed, but after a little extra exertion always got free. There were four floors above and two underground. The latter are the bargain basements. London does not boast of any skyscraper buildings. On the top floors here I found restaurants, restrooms, a theatre where a show was going on, a cat and dog show, barber shop, smoking rooms, and on one flat a Japanese garden, with an artificial lake of goodly proportions in the center and native Japanese women sitting in the garden, making rugs, etc. and teaching the art. These stores carry practically every line of goods saleable in London. After a couple of hours in Selfridges store, I think, in that time, I had only explored a small part of the whole. I was carried by the surging crowd to the bargain basement. Here I bought a bathrobe for 37 shillings and saw many men buying good felt hats for two pounds, six shillings.

After having dinner at the Cosmo Hotel, which was a favourite spot with me in which to dine, I attended a review named *The Street Singer* with a wonderful performer named Arthur Tracey, in the Lyric Theatre. Last night, Madam Tussaud's Wax works, with its chamber of horrors, Napoleon, and other priceless relics, which I visited two days ago, was almost entirely destroyed by fire.

March 20 (Friday)

This forenoon, I stood outside Buckingham Palace and saw King George and Queen Mary drive out on their way to Victoria Station, where the King was to board the train for the first stage of his journey to Marseilles, where he will join his yacht for a health cruise on the Mediterranean. The Londoners, or perhaps I should say the English, have a great reverence for royalty, as on this particular morning large crowds lined the streets to see the King go by. There was great cheering and one need not be very observant to see the look of loyalty and affection (some may perhaps call it servility) in the faces of the assembled gathering. After calling at my tailors, I did some further sightseeing until noon, when I met Mr. Bremner by appointment and together we lunched. In the afternoon I called on Mr. Victor Gordon,[24] Newfoundland High Commissioner, at his office on Victoria Street. From there to see Colonel Nangle,[25] whose offices were in the same street.

I enjoyed a short talk with both men and heard some late Newfoundland news. At 5:30 p.m. went to Harrington & White's office and met Mr. Hoole, the manager. I told Bremner that I was

Holyhead, a small island in Wales, off the west coast of Anglesey, has served from time immemorial as the chief port for passenger service and mail between England and Ireland. Here we see a ferry about to depart from the customs house at the end of the sea wall and marine yard. It was sea walls such as this that inspired my father to demand a breakwater for Bay de Verde on his return from Europe. It took about 20 years for his dream to be realized. (Encyclopedia Universal)

leaving London for Dublin tomorrow. He, with two others of his coworkers and myself, left the office at 6:00 p.m. and proceeded to the sampling of scotch in more than one saloon, the intention, I suppose, being to drink the parting glass or glasses. At about 8:00 p.m., Mr. Bremner, who like the rest of us, had drunk not wisely, but too well and who is a married man, probably realizing that discretion is the better part of valour, hailed a taxi, bid me a fond and affectionate goodbye, which I heartily reciprocated and hied himself to the bosom of his family. In the company of my two new friends I went, at their invitation, to the Junior Constitutional Club and had dinner, after which "well who knows?"

How I accomplished the homeward trek is a secret that my then over-inebriated brain blotted out and has since refused to reveal. I negotiated it, however, and was informed next day, by the night porter who was on duty in reply to my enquiry, that I had arrived alone around midnight, came in and proceeded to the elevator and thence to my room. This was my first time to get "non compis mentis" on the trip. [My father was to admit in later years that this was the only occasion in his life when he got drunk.]

DUBLIN

March 21 (Saturday)

Went to Euston Station and took the train at 8:30 a.m. for Dublin, by way of the ferry from Holyhead. The day was fine and warm and I greatly enjoyed the scenes along the railway. At Conway we passed the ruins of a very large castle [Conway Castle]. We came through Wales, passing large flocks of sheep along the track, for which the Welsh are famous and saw many ponies.

Arrived at Holyhead at 2:15 p.m. This is a very narrow harbour and is made safe by a sea wall. After placing one of my grips in the parcel room to remain until my return, as I did not wish to have excess luggage for my short trip to Ireland, I boarded the cross channel boat S.S. *Scotia*, which was berthed at the pier on which the train stopped. About 30 feet separated the boat from the train. At 2:30 p.m., or as soon as mails, passengers and baggage were onboard, which I may say was done very expeditiously, we left. The *Scotia* is a fine boat, about the size of Bowring's S.S. *Silvia* at home. She is a passenger and mail boat exclusively, nicely appointed and has a speed of 23 knots.

I paid two pounds, six shillings and three pence for my ticket from London to Dublin by third-class train and first-class steamer. Most people travel third-class rail here. There are only first- and third-classes; no second – why, I don't know. The third-class, except in rush times when the trains are crowded, is very comfortable. It was blowing strong on the Irish Sea and very cold with snow squalls, but the water was smooth.

We arrived at Kingston at 5:10 p.m., in less than three hours, covering the 64 miles that separate Kingston, Ireland from Holyhead, England. Kingston Harbour is made by a sea wall or mole, in fact none of the seaports visited by me were natural harbours, but were made safe for shipping by the ingenuity of man in erecting sea walls.[26]

I was now in the Island of Destiny, the land of my forefathers, and a feeling of pleasure and of pride unconsciously thrilled me. I boarded the Dublin and Southwestern Railway and left at 5:30 p.m. for Dublin and in about 20 minutes, I was deposited on the platform of the Westland Row Station, in the historical city of Dublin. Motor cars, horse carriages, jaunting cars and hackney coaches were lined up for hire. I engaged one of the Irish jaunting cars, to take me to my hotel. When I climbed to the top of this vehicle the humourous spirit of the Irish race must have permeated me, for I, without any apparent reason, gave vent to my feelings with a loud laugh. This caused the driver to scrutinize me searchingly and probably he concluded he was driving a nut.

On arrival at my destination, the Standard Hotel, which is situated near St. Stephen's Green, the driver informed me that I owed him "three bob," which meant three shillings. This expression "three Bob" from the Irish driver again started me off into another good laugh. I might say, that before leaving any city I go to Thomas Cook & Sons, who have an office or offices in almost every city of importance in the world. They are the great touring agency, which conducts parties or individuals to any part of the world, and they are also bankers. At Cook's one may buy a ticket, whether by rail, steam or air, to any port or part of the world and at the same price charged by the railways, steamships or airlines. On these tickets Cook's gets a commission, which is their profit. They will tell you what hour you are to leave, when you will arrive at your next stop and recommend a hotel to you if asked to do so. If this is not sufficient, at almost every railway, air or steamship terminal in cities of importance throughout the world where tourists are accustomed to stop off in numbers, you will find a Thomas Cook & Sons man, with his name on his cap, whose business it is to know your language and reply to any questions and render all assistance possible to any who may need it.

I engaged a room at the Standard Hotel at nine pounds, six shillings with breakfast two pounds, six shillings, lunch two pounds and dinner three pounds – a total of 17 pounds – with tips this amounts to about $4.50 per day. After having dinner, I bought a guide book and map of the city and went for a long walk. As it was very cold tonight, the walk was not as enjoyable as it might have been. I saw many interesting sights, but although I walked through Grafton and O'Connell Streets, two of the principal streets of the city, I saw very little of the glare of Piccadilly Circus or the Paris boulevards.

March 22 (Sunday)

After partaking of an appetizing and substantial breakfast, the main ingredients of which were Irish ham, eggs and butter, I attended 9:00 a.m. mass at the Catholic University Chapel. The University is quite large and is in a different street from the chapel. In his time, Cardinal Newman was rector here.[27] His bust is in the chapel. After mass I walked to O'Connell Bridge, and saw the O'Connell monument, the pillar erected in honour of Admiral Lord Nelson, an Irishman, and statues of many of Ireland's patriotic sons, a number of which, adorn the streets of

TRAVEL DIARY OF JAMES O'NEIL

One of the earliest photos taken in Ireland, this view from the main bridge over the River Liffey, shows the enormous crowds who turned out in Dublin in 1875 to celebrate the centenary of the birth of the great Daniel O'Connell, "the liberator." An Irish political leader of enormous charisma and power, it was pressure by O'Connell that led to the Catholic Emancipation Act of 1829, which also emancipated Catholics in Newfoundland. In the photo, looking up Sackville Street, Nelson's Column and part of the portico of the General Post Office can just be seen. (National Museum of Ireland)

Dublin. I walked along the banks of the Liffey River which winds itself through the city and went down to the port or harbour front, where I had my first glimpse of Dublin Bay which is famous in song and story.

Passed by many docks, some of them being in locks off the Liffey, to which vessels get, by bridges being turned or raised. Moles or sea walls protect the port from the sea. Afterwards I walked back to Butt Bridge, which is the furthest one down toward the port. Crossed over and walked up the street on the river bank on the opposite side and at 12:30 p.m. entered St. Augustine's Church, in the middle of mass. The singing was very good and it was packed with a very devout gathering. People appear to have a great grip of the old faith, or vice versa, here. From there went to St. Audeon's church, but it was full and many were standing outside as a mission was being conducted.

Walked through the grounds of Dublin Castle and what thoughts flitted through my mind, as I went round those yards that actually teem with historical associations. This pile, which dates back to the thirteenth century, is now the law courts of the Free State government. It was at all times the centre of English power in Ireland and for centuries the name Dublin Castle was synonymous with oppression and misrule.

Visited St. Patrick's Cathedral which I thought was Roman Catholic, but found it Episcopalian [Church of England]. This church was founded in 1190 and had a very chequered career. It was once used by Cromwell as a stable. Dean Swift [author Jonathan Swift of *Gulliver's Travels*] who was dean of the cathedral from 1713 to 1725, and whose pulpit is here and Mrs. Johnson (Stella), whom Swift immortalized, are buried near the entrance. In the vaults, which I visited, lie the remains of Lord Edward Fitzgerald,[28] who with Wolfe Tone[29] was a leader of the United Irishman's Rebellion of 1798. Close by is St. Patrick's insane or mental asylum,

TRAVEL DIARY OF JAMES O'NEIL

Michael Collins, the charismatic Irish leader of Sinn Fein, was born in 1890. He was the first person to effectively organize and use guerilla warfare in Europe. He forced the British to sue for peace in Ireland. A treaty was worked out, separating Ulster, which he urged the Irish people to accept. In 1921, he joined Arthur Griffith in setting up the Irish Free State. Collins was assassinated in 1922 when ambushed by Irishmen opposed to the Free State. (Independent Newspapers - Dublin)

NO NEED TO WEAR RUBBERS

The Four Courts, Dublin home of the Irish National Archives. Winston Churchill's ultimatum to Collins to surrender his IRA Headquarters in the Four Courts was ignored. The British then bombarded the place, reducing the building to ruins. This action destroyed the nation's archives. The priceless records of centuries were showered among the nearby streets in charred fragments. This loss has retarded research in Ireland to this day. (Manchester Evening News)

founded by Dean Swift. This witty dean has satirized his own benefaction in those words:

He left the little wealth he had,
to build a house for fools and mad,
to show one satiric touch
no nation wanted it so much.

There were many old monuments and tombs, as well as a great profusion of old battle flags, some of which are in tatters, adorning the walls.

From St. Patrick's I went to the City Hall. The circular entrance hall witnessed the mourning of thousands around the biers of the great fighters for Irish freedom who were waked there. Among those were O'Donovan Rossa[30] and Parnell, and in quite recent years Arthur Griffith, the first president of the Irish Free State, and Michael Collins.[31] From here I wended my way to College Green. This is a fine open square, surrounded by extensive and prosperous looking buildings.

The Bank of Ireland, formerly the old Irish Parliament, which is looked upon as a gem of architecture, is here. In fact this section is the commercial hub of the city. In the centre of the Green is the equestrian statue of King William of Orange, popularly called King Billy. I might add, in passing I was informed that on the spot this monument had been destroyed on two or three occasions during the troubled times, but was always replaced.

In this vicinity were held many historic gatherings. The late Michael Collins, more familiarly known to his countrymen as Mick Collins, made his last public speech shortly before his death, standing beneath this statue in College Green. Here too is the statue of Henry Gratten.[32] At the head of the square or Green is Trinity College with its wealth of Celtic treasures, including the famous *Book of Kells*, the most ornate of Irish manuscripts, which is the work of Irish monks and is as fresh and its colours as bright today, as when it left the hands of those pious men who designed it, probably in the eighth century. There are also many other priceless manuscripts.

On the streets are to be seen many Free State soldiers. In their uniforms of dark green with tan boots and tan leather leggings, all carrying slight canes, they present an attractive and smart appearance. I saw these soldiers on guard at the Bank, at Dublin Castle and other important points. As yet Ireland's internal troubles are not completely ended. I saw ruins of many noble buildings destroyed in the recent fighting [Easter Rebellion], among them the Post Office and Customs House.[33] These latter were two splendid piles lavishly adorned outside with statuary, ornamental stone and masonry. Some of the walls of both are still standing, mute reminders of the hell through which Ireland wallowed to gain some form of independence for her downtrodden people.

The pubs are open for business from 2:00 p.m. to 5:00 p.m. on Sunday, and I want to say that two that I visited were hives of industry. At 4:00 p.m. I went to the Church of St. Myra and from there paid a second visit to St. Audeon's church, where the mission was being conducted and where I heard a very instructive sermon, the first for a long time. It was not possible to hear the sermon as well as one would wish because children and even infants in arms displayed their vocal abilities quite freely. Outside the church was a stall in which religious articles were for sale. The closing of the mission was very impressive. All participants held lighted candles above their heads and renewed their promises and resolutions; after which the papal blessing was given, followed by benediction of the Blessed Sacrament.

After leaving the church, I came to the ruins of the Four Courts, once a Dominican Priory, but on the Suppression of the Monasteries by Henry VIII it was parcelled out to the friends of the invaders. King James II held a parliament here. The place is on the banks of the Liffey and contained, as its name implies, "the Courts" and was a building of great dimensions and beauty before its partial destruction.

During the civil war of 1922 it became the headquarters of the Republican Army. As a result of a bombardment of the "Free State Troops" and an ensuing explosion, it was practically destroyed. Rory O'Connor and Cathel Burga,[34] Republican Army rebel leaders, with about 60 of their men, were taken alive from the ruins and afterwards lined up and shot at Mountjoy Jail by order of their fellow countrymen of the Free State government. These executions were essential if law and order were to be preserved. More important than the destruction of the building is the immeasurable loss sustained to Ireland by the burning of the Records Office with its irreplaceable and priceless records.

The place was surmounted by a dome, which did not collapse. When I was there, workmen were repairing and strengthening it. The heavy barbed wire, which was used around the building for defence purposes by the rebels, was still in position. Marks of shots are to be seen in the walls of many buildings along the streets. Poor old Dublin does not look very prosperous. Its streets are poorly lighted. Compared to London, there are few motorcars on its streets and taken as a whole, it was very evident that the ruthless hand of adversity had been against it. Cabs and jaunting cars predominate as vehicles of transport.

I have met many poor people and a few beggars, but have not yet seen any painted dolls, although at the hotel last night some of the female guests smoked. Nelson's Pillar [afterwards blown up by the IRA March 8, 1966] is a very conspicuous landmark which stands in the centre of O'Connell Street opposite the ruins of the Post Office, blown up at the start of the Easter Rebellion. A small

The jaunting-cart seen here, with two lady passengers, stands outside the National Library. It was a favourite mode of travel in Dublin. My father preferred hiring and riding in them, during his Dublin visit, to the enclosed cabriolets (horse-drawn cabs). In 1904, there were some 656 cabriolets in Dublin. Sir William Orpen recalled, that by about 10:00 p.m. at night "every decent driver was fairly well-laden with alcohol." (National Library of Ireland Archives)

charge admits one to the top of the monument, from which a fine view may be had towards the bay. O'Connell's monument is not far from this pillar.

Things are expensive here and the people are heavily taxed. Guinness stout sells for eight pence here, in the city of its manufacture, the high price being due to a heavy excise duty. I have bought it in England for much less. Today I priced John Jamieson's Whiskey, which is manufactured in this city. It sells for 16 shillings and eight pence, or about four dollars per bottle. This high price is also due to the heavy excise duty on luxuries. The street names are put up in both English and Irish. Some of the stores have the names of the proprietors over the doors in Irish. The brogue is

TRAVEL DIARY OF JAMES O'NEIL

The General Post Office Building on O'Connell Street, Dublin, where the Easter Rebellion of 1916 began. It was occupied Easter Monday as the provisional government's headquarters by signers of the proclamation of the Irish Republic and other rebels. Patrick Pearse then read the proclamation from the steps. The populace, generally unaware of these events, paid them little heed until Tuesday when British troops and artillery opened fire, reducing the building to ruins and arresting and executing the rebel leaders. To the right is Nelson's Pillar, which was blown up by Irish Republicans in 1966. (National Archives of Ireland)

very much in evidence. On my way to the hotel, I had a nice walk through St. Stephen's Green. This is a nice park of 22 acres, with two artificial lakes in which were many swans, ducks, etc. It is a gift to the city from Sir Arthur Guinness, of brewery fame.

NO NEED TO WEAR RUBBERS

March 23 (Monday)

Took street car (a double decker) from O'Connell Bridge to Phoenix Park gate. On the way I passed the O'Connell Barracks and the graveyard of the Croppie Boys (those who died in the rebellion of 1778). Drove through the park on a hackney. For the latter mode of conveyance, I appear to have developed a weakness. The park is two and 3/4 miles through and contains 1,750 acres. Much of it is wooded and a large part of it laid out in flower beds. Nice walks, lakes and valleys are in this enclosure.

The Liffey flows at your feet as it were quite near the park and adds to its beauty. There is a very interesting collection of animals in the zoo here. Lion taming is a specialty, and many tame deer roam its expanse. A stone pillar, or obelisk, standing 250 feet high, raises its lofty head here to the memory of Wellington, the Iron Duke, who, like Nelson, was born in Ireland. The base of the Wellington monument is decorated with bronze figures (made from captured guns) of scenes in his battles.

The official residence of the British appointed Governor General was here, as are the military hospital and other buildings. Phoenix Park has much historical data connected with it. My next stop from here was Glasnevan Cemetery and what an interesting spot. Just inside the gate of God's Acre is a nice chapel. The usual assortment of varied marble monuments, stones, slabs and vaults is here.

Visited the graves of Michael Collins and Arthur Griffith, whose deeds and activities for Irish freedom, but not of the extreme sort, are still fresh and verdant in our memories; also the graves of Cathel Burga and Harry Boland, two leaders of the rebels against the newly constituted government, who paid for their zeal with their lives by being executed in 1922.

TRAVEL DIARY OF JAMES O'NEIL

An Irish immortal, Patrick Pearse, born in 1879, educator, and president of the fashionable St. Enda's Boy's school was a famous patriot, active in the Gaelic League. Pearse led Irish forces at the Dublin Post Office in the Easter Rebellion of 1916 (See endnote 33), which ended in 1922 with the creation of the Irish Free State. When the rising at the Post Office collapsed in 1916, he was arrested, imprisoned and shot with the other rebel leaders. (National Museum of Ireland)

The Republican or rebel section in the cemetery, is separated from the Free State plot, so that even in death those over-zealous souls who sacrificed everything: home, family, even life itself, for the cause which both sides thought was in the best interest of their beloved Erin, lie forever in separated graves. Collins' grave was surrounded by those of Free State soldiers who died in action, whereas Cathel Burga's was encompassed by the bodies of hot-blooded youths, whose one burning ambition was to have Ireland a nation and who had freely given their precious lives for what was to them, the greatest of causes. To further emphasize the separation of the two opposing factions in death, I read over one grave this inscription: "Brutally murdered by the Free State Troops." No monuments are yet erected to any of the above mentioned, but innumerable glass cases, filled with artificial flowers and cards, are everywhere around.

Michael Collins, when he received the fatal wound which ended his very promising career, held the very dangerous and unenvi-

Charles Stuart Parnell, the great Irish nationalist leader, united diverse elements of Irish patriots. Elected to the British Parliament, he agitated for, and achieved, reforms in Ireland. When named correspondent in a divorce suit in 1889 by the husband of his inamorata, Kitty O'Shea, he met with strong opposition from Irish Catholic clergy. He soon lost his all political influence, leading to his death in 1891, a broken man (See endnote 35). My father, quite moved by his visit to Parnell's grave in Glasnevin, always treasured a flower he picked there and pressed. (Radio Times Hulton Picture Library)

able position of commander-in-chief of the Free State Army. After the death of Collins, Richard Mulcahy was immediately appointed to the same position. I was informed by a cemetery official that the morning following the burial of Collins a card was found on his grave which read "Move over Mick and make room for Dick." Comment is unnecessary.

Visited Parnell's grave.[35] He has no marble monument, but a small iron cross stands sentry over the noble remains. On a tablet near his grave is the following: "The memory of Parnell and his splendid services will last 'til our race perishes and our history is forgotten."

The outstanding object of interest here is the tomb of Daniel O'Connell, the great liberator, in the crypt beneath the round tower. This tower, which is Ireland's monument to one of her greatest sons, stands 80 feet high. Visitors are allowed to ascend to the top. The crypt, or vault, which I visited is quite spacious and on its white marble walls are inscribed in letters of gold O'Connell's last pious hope and wish, or as many call it, his last will and testament. It was made on his deathbed in France as he was on a journey to Rome. The soul stirring words, which came from a loyal son of the Catholic church are: "My heart to Rome. My body to Ireland. My soul to God."

His casket, which is a light oak colour, is resting on two stands in the centre of the chamber. Connected with this chamber by a door is another room in which lie three or four coffins of O'Connell's relatives, piled one on the other. Surrounding the base of the monument is a circular ditch, whose walls stand about 12 feet high. Those walls are all taken up with vaults with iron doors that are filled with coffined bodies and with monuments above. There is an iron door of rods to O'Connell's tomb, and even from the outside the casket is in plain view.

God's Acre is well looked after and in summer must be very beautiful. Its well-cared surroundings and peaceful glens are a fitting resting place for the hallowed remains that here await the call of the last trumpet. From here I walked to Mountjoy Jail and surveyed its exterior, and although I tried to gain admittance, I did not succeed.

Inside the walls of this austere looking place, Cathel Burga and Harry Boland, with about 60 of their followers were lined up and shot in 1922. The bodies of the executed ones were first buried in the prison grounds, but were afterwards disinterred and transferred to Glasnevan. I was told this funeral of 60 or more of Ireland's brave young sons was the largest ever seen in the streets of Dublin.

Took a streetcar to College Green and thence to Christ Church Cathedral. This is now a Protestant church, but its predecessors – built, destroyed and rebuilt many times – were Roman Catholic churches. Saint Lawrence O'Toole, who was canonized about a half century after his death, was the first bishop to be consecrated in Ireland, and is buried in a chapel dedicated to him in this church. I saw a heart-shaped casket, or urn, hanging here, which is thought to contain the heart of St. Lawrence O'Toole. In the nave is a monument to Richard Strongbow, Earl of Pembroke, who captured Dublin in 1170. His effigy has legs crossed, which means he was twice or thrice a crusader. His tomb is in the crypt along with those of some of Ireland's Kings. One of the walls of this church is more than three feet out of plumb, due to the ground sinking, but it has been strengthened and supported from the outside and has been thus for more than a century.

There is a seat here for royalty, also one for the Lord Mayor. There are no longer Lord mayors in Ireland, this functionary being abolished. The last person to hold this office was a Roman Catholic. This church, like many other buildings in Dublin, has had a very eventful career. The crypt, which I visited with a guide, dates back to 1033. In it are the old stocks. Tunnels underground, some of which were a half-mile long, once connected this place with St. Michan's Church, Dublin Castle and under the Liffey in other directions.

These tunnels were used as avenues of escape in the days of the ruthless religious persecutions, when many were forced to burrow in the earth in order to preserve their lives. Those tunnels are now closed or fallen in, but the entrances to them seen here are mute evidence of their existence. Bobby Burns, the great Scottish poet, after walking through one of them composed a ballad and compared the tunnel through which he had passed to hell. An army officer and his dog once went to explore one of these tunnels, and while he was in someone closed the heavy door. Some months after his remains were found, but his body and that of his dog had been eaten by rats.

From Christ Church, I crossed the river to St. Michan's (Protestant) Church. This was built by the Danes in 1095 and its original tower is still standing. It is situated quite near the Four Courts, so near in fact that the force of the explosion in 1922, which practically destroyed the latter, broke a large stained glass window in the end of the church; the opening being temporarily boarded up when I visited it. In the little graveyard of the church are buried Dr. Lucas Oliver Bond and other leaders of the Croppie Boys, in the '98 Rebellion. I was shown a plain marble slab here, under which is said to lie the body of Robert Emmett, who immortalized himself in his speech to the court when he was condemned to death. However, the claim to this being his burial place has not been substantiated. The church organ is 210 years old and is claimed to be the oldest and sweetest in Ireland.

There are 40 vaults in the crypt beneath the church, some of which contain as many as forty coffins in plain view. These vaults are, in my opinion, among the wonders of the world. For centuries, bodies have been buried here without being embalmed. The coffins are simply placed one on top of the other in the vaults, or rooms, and after centuries those coffins or caskets moulder away to dust and collapse, the whole pile of coffins sometimes falling, but the bodies are still wonderfully well-preserved. The skin on these corpses appears to be of the consistency of leather and is a dark brown in colour. The ears, lips and teeth appear to be intact and, I am told, in some of the bodies that have been opened up, the heart and lungs were to be seen. In those vaults filled with the dead, some of which have been buried only recently, there is positively no offensive odour.

Different theories have been advanced as to why the bodies do not decompose here, one of which is that a grove of oak trees once grew in this place and the preventative is in the roots of the oak trees. Another is that the air in the vaults is so dry that no microbe can thrive, except a species of cannibalistic spider which grows to a very large size. Their webs stretch from the bottom to the top of some of the vaults. Bodies are still buried here and I saw coffins or caskets 30 and 40 years old in almost perfect condition on which the brass plates were not even tarnished. No flowers are allowed in these vaults. On one occasion, when the bodies of two long lost and well-beloved patriots were discovered here, the populace brought flowers, placed them in the vault alongside and on top of their caskets, with the result that the dampness contained in the flowers caused the destruction of practically everything in the cell. To preserve the bodies in question, the caskets were put in lead containers. This was called to my attention by a guide, and I was shown and I saw the piles of decayed debris in this cell.

From St. Michan's I crossed back over the river and walked past the Guinness Brewery. It is surrounded by a high stone wall. Opposite it on the riverfront is the long narrow shipping pier with its dozen or more cranes. I also visited several Roman Catholic churches, of which St. Peter's Philsborough was a gem. It had a mosaic setting round the chancel, while its altars and pulpits were things of beauty. I saw part of the Dublin fire brigade today, in their scarlet shirts and steel helmets.

This is the city where Peterson's tobacco pipes and Jacobs celebrated biscuits are made. At the Standard Hotel, where I am a guest, smoking is not allowed in the dining-room. This is the first dining-room I have been in to date where this rule prevails. Coffee is served in the lounge after dinner. This is also the first hotel where I have seen a napkin ring, and I noticed guests folding their napkins and placing them in the rings after meals. At all other hotels I have visited, fresh napkins were supplied at every meal. Another noticeable thing here is that no keys are given guests for their bedrooms. All rooms are open. I paid 2 pounds, 10 shillings, (68 cents) today, for a two ounce tin of sliced Edgeworth tobacco. On inquiring, I found that Johnny Walker, Red Label Whiskey, sells for 16 pounds, about $3.85.

TRAVEL DIARY OF JAMES O'NEIL

March 24 (Tuesday)

Visited the National Library and from there to the Natural History Museum in Merrion Square. The National Gallery contains a splendid collection of Irish paintings and statuary. Many original letters of O'Connell, Gratten and others are there. Also, there is a rich collection of old china, porcelain, tapestry, relics of the stone age, bronze age, early iron period, etc.

Numerous interesting articles of early Irish ecclesiastical art, harps antique and modern, state coaches and 1,001 other items here, can scarcely be seen owing to the Free State Senate occupy-

Since 1759, Guinness has been brewed in Dublin. This photo of the brewery's racking shed, taken around 1890, shows coopers at work. Coopers were among the most skilled tradesmen of their day and made the wooden casks in which the Guinness beer and stout was shipped. Tours of the brewery have been conducted since the mid-nineteenth century and end in the tap room where visitors may taste free samples of the famous brews. (Guinness Brewery Archives)

ing part of the building – which they are soon to vacate to go to Leinster House, the display is much too crowded.

Between the library and the museum is the Dáil[36] or Free State House of Parliament. Soldiers are on guard here. Leinster House, in which the Dáil is housed, was formerly the town house of the Duke of Leinster and afterwards of his heir, Lord Edward Fitzgerald. It is surrounded by an extensive well-kept lawn. On the opposite side of Leinster House is Merrion Square. This is a very fine residential section. A temporary cenotaph to the memory of President Griffith and General Michael Collins faces this square.

My next visit was to the Guinness brewery. A uniformed guide is provided here who conducts sightseeing parties through the different buildings and makes any desired explanations. He intelligently answers questions from the visitors. Guinness stout is known and consumed practically throughout the civilized world. This is a most interesting plant and covers 50 acres. There are 4,000 people employed here, about 300 of whom are coopers [barrel-makers]. None of the output is bottled here. All is shipped out in oak casks, the bottling being done by other firms, such as S & J Burke, etc. There are 24 circular vats in which the malt is boiled. Those boilers hold 200 barrels each.

Malt and hops are the only ingredients used, except water. Since no country in the world is thought capable of curing hams with an equally toothsome flavour to those cured and smoked in Ireland, so no country in the world can produce stout to compare with the Dublin stout made at Guinness Brewery. There are 16 fermenting tanks of wood holding 1,600 barrels each, in one brewery alone. On the way to those tanks the mixture passes through refrigerators and the yeast is added. As soon as fermentation is complete (which is in two or three days), it is pumped to open vessels to cool and is skimmed of the froth or yeast. From here, it goes by gravity to the storage vats. These are immense oak casks. They hold about 100,000 gallons each. It takes a half mile of very heavy iron hoop to construct one of those casks. Guinness sales in 1914 were 105 million gallons. There is a cleaning department where from 15 to 20 thousand returned casks are cleaned and sterilized daily, and one of the best paying jobs in the establishment is smelling the bungs [stoppers] of those casks to see if they are sufficiently sweet to be refilled. Nineteen thousand, of various sizes, are filled in an eight hour day.

Our last call was to the sampling room where we were given to drink samples of the three grades of stout which they manufacture here, namely porter, extra stout and foreign stout. The foreign stout is much stronger than the other grades. This latter grade is made solely for export and is especially manufactured to stand up and retain its flavour on ocean voyages and in any climate. In addition to horses and motor trucks, about 20 steam wagons or locomotives with trailers are used here, delivering the manufactured stout and by-products to the shipping quay and elsewhere. In pre-war days, stout of a higher alcoholic strength than is now supplied was sold for two pence a bottle. Due to government interference, the same size bottle is now sold for eight pence in Ireland. Whiskey, which was sold for four pence a glass before the war, is now one shilling and eight pence. This increased price is caused by higher excise duties, which is particularly noticeable here on all goods of the luxury class.

The amount paid by Guinness for excise duty on stout in 1919 was approximately five million pounds, or about 24 million dollars, which is equal to the total revenue received by our Newfoundland government in about two and a half years; or to put it another way, it is equal to about £25,000, or $120,000 every working day. About 12,000 persons depend on the brewery for their support.

From Guinness', I went to the pipe factory of Kapp & Peterson. I was shown the briar from which the well-known Peterson's Patent

NO NEED TO WEAR RUBBERS

Leinster House, outside which a dozing cabbie awaits a fare, was built as the Dublin residence of the FitzGeralds, Dukes of Leinster. Lady Pamela, wife of Lord Edward FitzGerald, presided there as chatelaine, prior to her husband's involvement in the United Irishman's Rebellion of 1898, in which he was arrested and died in prison. Pamela was born Anne Simms in Fogo, Newfoundland, the illegitimate daughter of Nancy Simms, a woman of the place. Leinster House is today the home of Ireland's Parliament the Dáil. (National Archives of Ireland)

Pipes are made and which is imported from France. The briar trees which I saw here are quite small, but the briar for the pipes is imported in small blocks, only of sufficient size to make one pipe. I followed the pipe through the different processes of manufacture, from the block of wood until it was finished, polished and ready for the smoker. I was shown large chunks of meerschaum and amber, which later would be used for making pipes and stems.

I noticed that motor trucks here use a sort of brush on their wheels so as not to splash pedestrians. My ticket to Liverpool, which I bought today, cost one pound, three shillings.

March 25 (Wednesday)

Went to mass at the Roman Catholic Pro Cathedral. Found the church packed with devout worshippers waiting for the 11:00 a.m. mass. This, I might add, is the Lenten season. From a cursory glance around the worshippers and a comparison with the indifference shown by congregations seen in churches and cathedrals recently visited by me in other countries, I have not any doubt that here in the Republic of Ireland is to be seen genuine devotion to the faith of our fathers. There was no music or singing at the mass, unless one were to estimate as such the cooing and crying of infants in arms who were brought here by loving parents to have the first instincts of religious fervour and longing instilled into their innocent and inquisitive little souls. From the large number of children I have seen, it struck me that race suicide [abortion] or contraception is unknown or unpracticed here. This cathedral is in a very congested locality. In size it is small and is also very dark. Neither its interior nor exterior is attractive.

From here, I went by bus to All Hallows College. This is an institution for educating priests and I was very pleased to find some

NO NEED TO WEAR RUBBERS

Daughter of a wealthy Sligo family, Constance Gore-Booth (See endnote 38) was praised in poetry by Yeats as second in beauty only to his paramour, the actress Maud Gonne. In Paris, at 31, Constance fell in love with and married Count Casimir Markiewicz, a Polish womanizer and landowner from the Ukraine. Through Maud Gonne, she met the revolutionary James Connolly, and instead of spending her time in feminine pursuits, she became his disciple and the leader of the 1916 rebellion. The photo shows her, when, in the words of Yeats, "young and beautiful she rode to harriers."

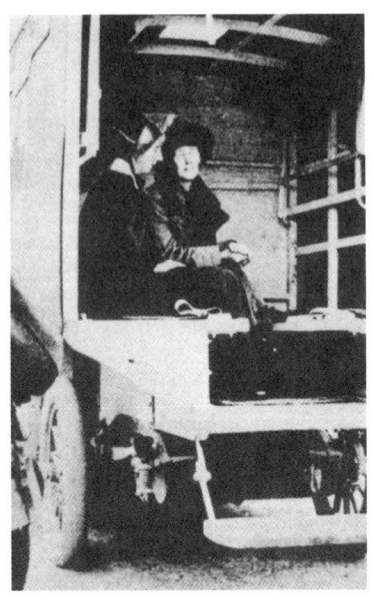

This other photo shows her as the Rebel Countess, seated in a Red Cross wagon, on her way to prison and execution, following her court-martial. Yeats wrote of her in Easter 1916, that she spent her days "in ignorant good will... until her voice grew shrill." She and de Verllera were eventually reprieved and given their freedom. When asked to take an oath to the British King at the time of her release from prison she refused saying, "How could I ever meet Paddy Pearce and Jim Connolly in the hereafter if I took an oath to the British King?" (National Museum of Ireland)

118

These cells in Dublin's Kilmainham Jail are now open to tourists as a sort of shrine. In them the leaders of the failed Easter Rebellion of 1916 were imprisoned. Following their courts-martial, all but two were taken outside and executed. Countess Markievicz occupied the first cell on the left, while other rebel leaders of the uprising: Pearse, Clarke, MacDiarmada, etc., filled the adjoining cells and those opposite. Gravely ill after an operation for appendicitis, the countess died, July 15, 1926. Her body lay in state in the capital's Rotunda. Her funeral, which was a vast demonstration of affection by the Irish people, included eight lorry loads of flowers. (Paul O'Neill)

sons of Terra Nova among the students. I had a chat with two of the inmates, the present Fathers Maher and Gibbs[37] and spent a most interesting hour in their company.

From here to the Municipal Galleries and St. Stephen's Green, thence to the Dáil, which was to be in session today and for which I had procured a pass by showing my passport, which, by the way, contained the good old Irish name O'Neil. A soldier took me inside to my seat and a few minutes after my arrival the members began to file in and the session commenced.

President William Cosgrove appeared to me an outstanding figure. He is a man about 40 or 45 years old, fair hair, tall and commanding. Blythe, who by the way is a Presbyterian, is Minister of Finance. He looks considerably older than the president. I had the pleasure during my stay of hearing the President speak on soldier's pensions, which was up for discussion, and he is a fluent and able speaker. Kevin O'Higgins, Minister of Justice, who was also present, is very youthful looking and is small of stature. Peter Hughes, Minister of Defence, who made a good speech, is an Episcopalian.

I was glad to see from the above demonstration that in this country, which is predominately Catholic, bigotry and religious intolerance, the great curse of many supposedly educated and cultured countries today, is undoubtedly unknown. Unquestionably, the above speaks volumes for the tolerance and fair mindedness of the people of Southern Ireland, and it is a crying shame that many other nations do not follow in the footsteps of this infant parliament in this respect. Deputy Johnson, leader of the opposition in the house, criticised the government and let no opportunity pass without jumping to his feet and heckling the speakers. I spent about two hours here, which I enjoyed immensely. A very obliging and affable gentleman, who sat next to me, pointed out the different celebrities, one of whom was the Countess Markievicz,[38] whose name is well known in many lands.

At 8:10 p.m., I left Westland Row Railway Station for Kingstown and at 8:50 p.m. was onboard the channel boat *Scotia* bound for Holyhead, which is actually a small island in Wales, and is the chief port for mail and passenger service between Dublin and Liverpool, to which it is linked. The boat was crowded with passengers, many of whom were clerics bound to Liverpool to attend the Grand National Steeplechase race.

It blew a gale while we were crossing and judging from the way the

TRAVEL DIARY OF JAMES O'NEIL

In the twin towers of the Royal Liver Building an important part of Liverpool's world famous waterfront, Liver birds (pronounced ly-ver) nest. This landmark, which greets ships arriving or departing Liverpool, was constructed by Edward VII in 1907-1911. For many years Newfoundland ships, such as the SS Newfoundland and the SS Nova Scotia docked at Liverpool. My father ended his journey on board the SS Sachem, *April Fool's Day 1925, which was on its regular sailing between St. John's and Liverpool.* (Encyclopedia Universal)

ship tossed, the sea was very rough. I might add that the night was very dark and no passengers were allowed on deck.

LIVERPOOL

March 26 (Thursday)

Arrived at Holyhead at 11:45 p.m. and after about a half-hour delay, boarded the train for Chester, where we arrived at 2:10 a.m. This was our first stop after leaving Holyhead. Here we changed for Liverpool and pulled out at 2:30 a.m. On arrival at Liverpool at 3:15 a.m. I went to the Northwestern Hotel, which is right at the

121

station and is owned by the railway, but could only get a room for more than one night owing to the Grand National Race coming off tomorrow. Hotel accommodation is at a premium. Retired to bed at 4:00 a.m. and remained there until 9:00 a.m.

My room for the four or five hours I used it, with no bath and no hot water, cost 10 pounds, six shillings, a rather expensive nod. On calling at the hotel office after breakfast, as instructed, I was informed that their rates were now two guineas a day. My breakfast cost four shillings, which with a tip or two, made my few hours somewhat costly. As things were too rich here for my blood, I took my grip and left and placed it in the parcel room of the railway station. I might add that all the Liverpool hotels have taken advantage of the vast crowds of people, who have come here for the race, and considerably increased their rates. On my way to Ireland, I placed one of my grips in the parcel room in Holyhead so that I would not have excess baggage to take over, and my intention was to pick up this valise on my way back.

I had a long walk along the waterfront and watched with interest, and no little pleasure, the constant stream of ships, large and small, steam and sail, coming and going, up and down the Mersey River, which is the extensive expanse of water on which this great seaport is built. This is a very busy port. It has more than 20 miles of docks, many of which are immense, and shipping from practically every country in the world that is bordered by the sea is to be seen here.

Traffic on the waterfront streets is very great and the tooting of the whistles of tugs and ships in the harbour is increasing night and day. Oh, but it is smoky here. The exteriors of the buildings, some of which are very fine structures, are black as tar. I passed a motor lorry stopped in a traffic jam, in which there were about 20 turbaned Turks who had just landed.

Went to the Furness Withy office at the Royal Liver Building[39] and met Mr. McGuinness, the manager, to whom I had a letter of introduction. I might add, that I bought my ticket to Newfoundland from Liverpool by S.S. *Sachem*, from Mr. Bremner in London, he being entitled to a broker's commission on the sale. On my arrival at Holyhead from Ireland, my valise had entirely escaped my memory, and I was well on the road to Liverpool before I thought of it. I gave to one of Mr. McGuinness's assistants, at his request, the receipt for the bag left at Holyhead, so that he may have it sent to me. On account of hotel rates being so high, I boarded the train at 3:00 p.m. and for three pounds, nine shillings went to Manchester, where I arrived at 3:45 p.m.

Booked at the Victoria Hotel at 10 pounds, six shillings for room only. Had dinner at a small hotel at two pounds, six shillings – also I had a glass of Dewars whiskey at one pound, eight shillings. This is a manufacturing city of great prominence and innumerable tall chimneys belch forth black smoke in all directions, which envelopes the city to such an extent it is not possible to see very far, and almost everything on the street is black.

March 27 (Friday)

Went to Cook's, withdrew 10 pounds, and bought a ticket for three pounds, nine shillings and returned to Aintree, a small town inland from Liverpool, where the Grand National Steeplechase horse race takes place today [this race is one of the most popular betting sports events of the year in the United Kingdom]. Left the railway station on a very crowded train at 11:00 a.m. and due to arrive at Aintree at 11:45 a.m., but owing to an accident on the line, in which an engine and tender left the rails and turned over we did not arrive until 12:40 p.m. It was but a short walk to the race course and the surging and hurrying mob, of which I was an insignificant unit, was soon at its destination.

123

I have never seen such a vast crowd in any one place, at any one time. It cost three pounds to get into the outside grounds, one got somewhat further for one pound, six shillings, and by parting with 10 pounds one had the privilege of climbing onto the grandstand with just a very faint hope of being sufficiently lucky to secure a seat, which I may add was a necessity and not a luxury, after the jostling one went through to get there. Bookmakers, with whom one could do his betting on the race, were around the field in their hundreds and a great din was occasioned by their continuous yelling.

The Steeplechase, the principal race of the day, is certainly a thriller. The horses and jockeys in their run, must jump fences, ditches, etc. I saw three noble animals fall with their riders, all of whom, luckily, escaped serious injury. Many times, jockeys are killed or seriously injured. The horse that won third place came in riderless, having thrown her jockey in a fall and got on her legs again to continue the race to the end. I was interested in a game, which was very much in evidence among the crowds, known as "three card monte." Not having a previous introduction to this game, I thought after observing it for awhile, that it was easy as pie to win a few pounds, but I found after a short acquaintance that if I did not shake my new friend, I would soon be high and dry on the rocks. Barnum says there is a sucker born every minute. He's right.

At 3:00 p.m. I left the field to try, with the help of His Majesty's police force – 500 of whom were in Aintree that day – to find my rightful railway station. I might say there are four or five stations, owned by different railway companies here. Whichever station I went to was the wrong one for me and apparently every one I asked for directions gave me a wrong tip. The crowds were dense. I got near a station platform, at which a train was standing and heard someone say "Next-stop Manchester." I jumped from the platform to the train, arriving back in Manchester at 5:45 p.m.

The day was fine, but somewhat cold with very little drunkenness in evidence. No betting was allowed at the track except that done through the bookmakers, and during the races aeroplanes continually soared over the field taking photographs. I went to a picture show called *The Terror* tonight. The seats in the theatre were nicely upholstered and comfortable and it was a good picture.

March 28 (Saturday)

Took 10:45 a.m. train to Liverpool and return, which cost seven pounds, six shillings and occupied about three quarters of an hour. In arriving at Liverpool today I got my grip, which was sent from Holyhead. It cost me 4 pounds, 10 shillings expressage. Attended a musical review in the afternoon, which was quite enjoyable. As this is the third and last day of the horse races, the crowds in the city are thinning and hotels are getting back to normal in both guests and prices.

Many stores here close at noon on Saturday. Spent some time in a large department store and an interesting hour in the fish, poultry, meat and vegetable market. I saw fresh cod priced at four pence a pound, Iceland dory cod, which was very salty, clean and white, at eight pence a pound, with a very thin, inferior salt cod at four pence, dry haddock at four pence and fresh cod roes at the same price. There was a great variety of fish. I noticed the skin on the fresh cod was whiter than that usually seen on Newfoundland cod. Went back to Manchester by a late train.

March 29 (Sunday)

Spent considerable time trying to find a Catholic church. Found one in a very wretched alley and attended mass. There was a mission here and a 40-hours Adoration of the Cross. A very old priest celebrated mass and there was great religious devotion in evidence and many communicants. In the afternoon, which was nice and fine, I covered much of the city. I attribute the cleanness of the atmosphere today to its being Sunday, which means the tall factory chimneys are idle. The liquor saloons open at 7:00 p.m. on Sundays. I visited a couple and found them well filled with male and female customers. All the hotels I visited when in Spain, France, England and Ireland have a licence, and the wine card is presented to one regularly at meals along with the menu.

March 30 (Monday)

Took the 8:25 a.m. train for Liverpool. Booked at Washington Hotel at eight pounds, six shillings for room and breakfast. Looked up the city directory at the hotel and found Arthur Pratt's[40] address, after which I called on him at his office and sample room. Did some buying in the afternoon and, after having dinner at the Washington, went out to a theatre.

March 31 (Tuesday)

Did some further buying today. At 1:00 p.m. Arthur Pratt and I went to a hotel and had lunch, after which I did more buying. At night I attended a movie show. Saw a picture of Edward, Prince of Wales embarking on HMS *Repulse* [a 26,500-ton Renown class battle cruiser, it was built by John Brown & Company in Clydebank, Scotland. One of two commissioned by the British Admiralty in 1915. Completed in August 1916]. It is wonderful the spontaneous applause, with which royalty or a picture of any member of the royal family is received in England. Patriotism and respect for and loyalty to the King, are very marked traits of the English. A picture of the Grand National Steeplechase race was shown and I think I saw it even better than from the grandstand at

Aintree. The admission fee was one pound, three shillings. There is but one showing, a long one, each night. Smoking was allowed here. I might add that for four pence I had been to an afternoon picture show in a beautiful theatre with plush upholstered seats.

Raining tonight, the first for some time. The fact is I have experienced very little rain since landing in Europe. Had dinner tonight at Lyons. At restaurants of this chain, which are quite universal and are of the style and about the same class as Child's restaurants in the United States. Patrons are requested not to give tips.

April 1 (Wednesday)

Went to Bowring's office at Castle Street and had a chat with Mr. Fred Bowring, Jr. The old firm of Bowring's do a very extensive shipping business. I spent the afternoon around the docks, which to me, were the main points of interest here, but as Home Sweet Home is now on my mind, sightseeing has lost its attraction for me.

I would like to have spent more time in Ireland, where I enjoyed every moment of my time and hated to leave so soon, but the SS *Sachem's* regular sailing day was put back, which I did not know until I arrived here.

April 2 (Thursday)

Called at Pratt's office again this morning, did some shopping, then back to the hotel and packed my grips, as passengers are to be on board the ship for Newfoundland at 1.00 p.m. At noon I boarded a taxi at the hotel and left for Homby Dock and in about half an hour I was onboard the good ship *Sachem*. The Liverpool docks, seen from the *Sachem* as we passed through them, are marvellous engineering feats, and in them were innumerable ships, some small while others were immense and of almost all nationalities.

Our ship proceeded through the docks accompanied by tugs. Bridges opened in front and closed behind us. The tugs in front and behind, whose power propelled us, kept up a continuous tooting or signalling. At 4:30 p.m. we were straightened out on the Mersey River. We dropped our pilot, said good-bye to the myriads of gulls for which this port is famous, and were off. I was now on the last stage of my journey to Newfoundland and home. In the words of Sir Walter Scott:

Breathes there the man, with soul so dead
Who never to himself hath said,
"This is my own my native land!"
Whose heart hath ne'er within him burned,
As home his footsteps he hath turned,
From wandering on a foreign Strand!

At afternoon tea in the saloon, I met Mrs. McGrath,[41] formerly of Osborne House, St. John's, as well as other Newfoundlanders. We were assigned our seats at table for the trip and settled down to life onboard ship. Dinner was served at 6:30 p.m. and at 9:00 p.m., feeling tired, I turned in.

April 3 (Friday)

At 7:00 a.m. the steward brought me a cup of tea in my bunk and at 8:00 a.m. I got up and dressed. This cup of tea at such an early hour was not wanted by me, but the bedroom steward was angling for a good tip at the end of the voyage. This is a beautiful morning, the sun is shining brightly and the sea is smooth. All hands turned up at breakfast, as there is scarcely a ripple on the water. We are passing the south coast of Ireland today and the ship is as steady as in port. About 25 passengers for St. John's are onboard and we are getting acquainted.

April 4 (Saturday)

It blew hard last night from the south, but as I slept soundly, I knew little of it. It is blowing quite strong today, with a little sea making. We made 233 miles in the last 24 hours. Today we are down to the routine of card playing in the main lounge, since cold shower baths are the order of the day on deck.

April 5 (Sunday)

Blowing half a gale, wind North. Ship rolling and pitching quite a bit. Cannot get on deck, which makes the time rather long. Some of the passengers are suffering from Mal de Mer. I consider the *Sachem* a very steady boat, as there is a nasty sea today and she is not doing so badly. About 5:00 p.m. my valises started to parade round my stateroom.

Our daily routine is 7:00 a.m. a cup of tea, with a biscuit or an apple, is served in our rooms. Breakfast follows at 8:30 a.m., then at 10:30 a.m. chicken broth is served in the smoke room. At 12:30 p.m. we have lunch. 4:00 p.m. there is afternoon tea in the dining room and at 6:30 p.m. dinner is served. Made 196 miles today.

April 6 (Monday)

Weather moderate and sea fairly smooth. Rain and fog. We did 236 miles.

April 7 (Tuesday)

Wind Southwest, light, but with a considerable head pitch. Most of the passengers not out to meals. Passed the *Sachem*'s sister ship *Digby* a few miles north of us, bound from St. John's to Liverpool, and we received a wireless report from her that there was no ice on the Newfoundland coast.

We have seen no ship since passing the Irish coast.

A news bulletin, which is received by wireless, is posted onboard every day, so we are kept in touch with the outside world.

April 8 (Spy Wednesday - the Wednesday of Holy Week)

Ship making poor progress. It is not very comfortable on deck, as there is a fairly heavy sea on the beam and the ship has a very noticeable list to port. Many passengers are absent from meals. We have two men stowaways, one of whom spent nearly three days in a ventilator. Made 193 miles, the least for any day since we left Liverpool.

April 9 (Holy Thursday)

Fairly moderate, made 198 miles. A concert was held in the dining room from 8:30 p.m. to 10:30 p.m.

April 10 (Good Friday)

Blowing strong Northwest in the morning. Ship is rolling and pitching considerably. Toward evening wind moderated somewhat and veered from the South. This morning it was much cold-er than usual on deck. Last night it was 45° F [8°C]. This morning it is 31°F [0°C]. Made 225 miles the last 24 hours to noon, and another 228 miles separate us from St. John's.

Everybody is happy today, as we expect to be at our journey's end tomorrow.

April 11 (Easter Saturday)

Arrived in St. John's at noon, nine days from Liverpool, making 64 days on my round trip. On this wet April morning, the thing that struck me very forcibly was the muddy streets; as from the day I landed at Alicante until today, I had no need to wear rubbers.

NOTES

(1) Tarifa, at the southernmost tip of Spain, is a charming town with a splendid castle. Its beaches attract watersports and windsurfing enthusiasts. The closest city, well known to tourists, is Algeciras.

(2) My father's spelling here is incorrect. *Die Walküre* is the opera in three acts by Richard Wagner. In Spanish the correct spelling for the opera's title would be *Las Valquirias*. The work is part of the Ring cycle and tells of Wotan, Brunhilde, Siegmund, Sieglinde and Fricka.

(3) This is Barcelona's highest point. Standing at the precipice of Tibidabo mountain, it holds many attractions and delights. The famous Church of the Sacred Heart, atop the mountain, was started in 1902 and is of neo-gothic design.

(4) H.R.H. Prince Arthur, Duke of Connaught, brother of King Edward VII and uncle of the then monarch King George V, officially opened Bowring Park in St. John's July 14th, 1914. When visiting the park some years ago with Rosemary Mercereau, daughter of Sir Richard Squires, she pointed out the Connaught Stone upon which is mounted a plaque to commemorate the opening of the park by the Duke. It has the word Humber carved at the back. Humber was the Squires' family pet, a Newfoundland dog named for the river on which Sir Richard encouraged the Bowaters to build their papermill. Rosemary told me the family came home one evening in their car, to find Humber lying in a pool of blood in their driveway at the western end of the park. She claimed he had been shot to death by one of her father's political enemies. Sir Richard had the dog buried in their garden with the stone bearing his name placed over his grave. It was later taken up by the city of St. John's, moved from Squires' property and used as a base upon which to install the Connaught plaque.

(5) According to my mother, the break in relations between my father and his travelling companion was brought about by Coleman's penchant for inviting ladies of the night back to the room they shared, a thing which my father, a man of moral integrity, strongly disapproved. After an exchange of words, they went their separate ways – Coleman to Genoa, my father to Paris.

(6) The Dreyfus trial was a famous case in which Captain Alfred Dreyfus (1859-1935) was accused of treason by France. His being both a Jew and an Alsatian is said to have weighed heavily with his bigoted judges, and he was sentenced to life imprisonment on Devil's Island. When evidence was discovered pointing to Major Ferdinand Esterhazy as the true villain, the case became a huge international political scandal, which involved Emile Zola. The author was sent to prison for his article *J'accuse*, in which he accused the authorities of framing Dreyfus, who was pardoned in 1906. In 1930, papers were published which conclusively proved his innocence.

(7) Marshall Ney (1769-1815) was characterized by Napoleon I as "the bravest of the brave." He covered the retreat from Moscow in 1812, was created a duke and later a prince by Napoleon, and raised to the peerage by Louis XVIII, whom he supported after Napoleon's abdication. On the return of the former Emperor from Elbe, he promised the King to bring Napoleon to Paris in a cage, but changed his mind and joined forces with "The Little Emperor." After Napoleon's defeat at Waterloo, Ney was tried for treason and shot by order of the house of peers.

(8) Horatio Kitchener, First Earl of Kitchener (1850-1916). A British field marshal, he re-conquered the Sudan as commander-in-chief of the Egyptian Army and became its governor general. In the South African War, he systematically denuded Dutch farms to conquer the Boers. As Secretary of War in World War I, he expanded the army from 20 to 70 divisions. When a ship on which

133

he was travelling (to confer with Tsar of Russia) was sunk under rather mysterious circumstances, Earl Kitchener drowned.

(9) John Rushworth Jellico, First Earl of Jellico (1859-1935), was the British admiral in charge of the Grand Fleet in World War I and as first sea-lord commanded at the battle of Jutland. He was afterwards Governor General of New Zealand from 1920-24.

(10) In World War I the Germans mounted a huge offensive which brought them within 37 miles of Paris. The city shuddered under the bombardment of "Big Bertha." This was a 420 mm (16.5-inch) howitzer used by German forces advancing through Belgium in 1914. The guns were nicknamed for the Krupp arms works matriarch, Bertha Krupp von Bohlen. The term "Big Bertha" is sometimes applied to the Krupp manufactured artillery piece of completely different design that shelled Paris in 1918 from the phenomenal range of 75 miles. This later weapon, however, is more commonly known as the "Paris Gun."

(11) The first act of this show consisted of a seemingly endless line of dancing girls, singers and actors, including Raimu, who began his career as a music hall extra at the Toulon Casino. He went on to star in many Paris shows and was, for a brief period, with the Comédie Française. A favourite with the Folies Bergère, he also starred with Pierre Fresnay in Marcel Pagnol's classic film trilogy *Marius*, *César*, and *Fanny*. In Act II there appeared the great beauty, Mistinguett, France's most popular music hall star between World War I and World War II, along with Maurice Chevalier. This legendary performer, born in Enghiem, France, April 5, 1875, was known for her humourous one-liners such as: "A kiss can be a comma, a question mark or an exclamation point. That's basic spelling that every woman ought to know." Chevalier said of her, "She had a way of moving, which was the pinnacle of grace, but she was more than loveliness alone – she was Paris, the symbol of gaiety and good humor and courage and heart."

(12) The Volsted Act of 1919 was an act that banned the sale of alcoholic beverages in the United States by the Eighteenth Amendment to the Constitution. It proved a disaster and led to uncontrolled bootlegging, as well as unparalleled drinking, until 1933 when prohibition was repealed by the Twenty-first Amendment.

(13) That evening the program consisted of three acts. In Act I, the lyric drama *Miarka* was performed by Yvonne Gall, one of the great sopranos of her day, and wife of conductor Henri Büsser, the close friend of Jules Massenet, who is said to have written his opera *Manon* for her. The dance poem, *Istar*, by Vincent d'Indy in Act II, starred the incomparable Russian dancer, Ida Rubenstein in the title role. She was the first to dance Zobeide in Rimsky-Korsakoff's *Sheherezade* in Paris. In the Casino show she appeared in a number of tableaux with the Casino Girls and Boys as well as with Raimu. Act III was a ballet with music by de Lully, *Le Triomphe de l'Amour*. It was directed by André Caplet.

(14) George Clemenceau (1841-1929). The French Premier was dubbed "the Tiger." His Sacred Union Cabinet was instrumental in achieving the Allied victory in World War I. He opposed President Woodrow Wilson at the peace conference, regarding the Treaty of Versailles as too lenient. However, he was defeated in the 1919 elections because of the French voters' moderate attitude towards Germany.

(15) Aristide Briand (1862-1932). Premier of France 11 times between 1909 and 1921. Originally a Socialist, he later was attacked by the left and right for his liberalism. As foreign minister, he was chief architect of the Locarno Pact and the Kellogg-Briand Pact. An advocate for international cooperation and a United States of Europe, he shared the 1926 Nobel Peace Prize with Gustav Stresemann, German Chancellor from 1923-1929.

(16) Arthur Bremner was a partner in the firm of Harrington & White (London). They were fish brokers representing several Newfoundland firms, such as Ryan's of Bonavista and Bremner & Grieve of Trinity. They are said to have saved the Ryan firm from bankruptcy during the Great Depression. Alexander Bremner is believed to have been a brother of Arthur Bremner. His partner, Walter Richardson Grieve, was a close relative of Walter Baine Grieve who ran Baine, Johnston and Company for fifty years. Both Grieves were friends of my father.

(17) Lord Roberts (1832-1914), First Earl Roberts of Kandahar. He forced the people of Afghanistan to accept British demands in 1897. Commanded all Indian forces from 1885 -1893, commander-in-chief in the Boer War, 1899 - 1900.

(18) Walter Rummel was a charismatic American pianist and composer who had a major career in Europe in the 1920s until his death in Bordeaux in 1953. His playing also led to friendships with King Leopold III of Belgium and his wife, Queen Elizabeth. Rummel was a window on his time, an American who lived through two world wars and mixed easily with the musicians, writers, artists, philosophers and politicians of his day.

(19) This American musical by Vincent Youmans was an enormous hit on both sides of the Atlantic. It contained a number of delightful songs, two of which have become popular standards, "I want to be Happy" and "Tea for Two." Youmans ranked with George Gershwin, Irving Berlin, Jerome Kern and Richard Rodgers as America's five greatest Broadway composers.

(20) Daniel O'Connell (1775-1847) is said to have been the greatest Irish political figure. In 1823, he founded the powerful Catholic Association, whose pressure led the British Government to proclaim the Catholic Emancipation Act of 1829. He urged repeal of Ireland's union with England and worked until his death to solve the Irish land question.

(21) Lord Charles George Gordon (1833-1885) was known as "Chinese" Gordon, for having served as British administrator and commander-in-chief of the Chinese Army that suppressed the Taiping Rebellion. While serving as Governor General of Egyptian Sudan, he tried to crush the power of the Mahdi and was killed in the siege of Khartoum in 1885. Popular indignation at his death was a partial cause of the fall of the Gladstone government in England that year.

(22) Harrods in Knightsbridge celebrated its 150th birthday in 1999. The store began in the mid-nineteenth century when Henry Charles Harrod opened a grocery shop nearby on Brompton Road. By concentrating on high quality goods and excellent service, rather than cheap prices, the shop was popular enough to begin expanding. Ayre's and Knowling's occupied two large buildings on the east corner of Water Street and Ayre's Cove. Knowling's, one of the largest department stores in St. John's, was eventually taken over by Ayre's.

(23) Selfridges in Oxford Street, like Harrods in Brompton Road, hardly needs any introduction. It's as swanky, plush and deep carpeted as ever, and its spectacular food halls alone are worth a visit. It stands out from the pack for fashion.

(24) Captain Victor Gordon began work in the St. John's branch of the Bank of Montreal and then studied law in England where he was called to the bar of Middle Temple. He served in World War I with the King's own Scottish Borderers and was severely wounded. In 1919, he was appointed secretary to the Newfoundland High Commissioner's Office, serving Sir Edgar Bowring. He was appointed High Commissioner to London in 1924, the year before my father called on him at his office in Victoria Street.

(25) Thomas Nangle, son of a St. John's tailor, was a Roman Catholic priest ordained in 1913, who enlisted in the Newfound-

land Regiment in 1915 and became its padre in France. He was promoted to the rank of lieutenant-colonel in 1917 while on a short furlough in St. John's. During his visit, Nangle, who was extremely popular, delivered a short talk on the war at the Casino Theatre. After the armistice, he worked as Newfoundland's representative on the Imperial War Grave's Commission. He negotiated with French landowners for the purchase of what became the memorial park at Beaumont-Hamel. After leaving the priesthood, about 1930, he married and moved to Africa where he farmed and became a Reform Party politician in Rhodesia. In 1933 he was elected to the Rhodesian parliament. Father Nangle's vestments and the chalice he used in the war were donated by his daughter to the city of St. John's.

(26) Having seen breakwaters throughout Europe, my father, on his return to Newfoundland, and knowing of the constant destruction caused by storms to fishing boats, schooners and stages in Bay de Verde, decided that the community needed a breakwater. He began immediately to campaign for the construction of one by the Commission of Government, but had little success until his friend from Northern Bay, Sir John Puddester, was made a commissioner. Together, they worked toward that goal, which was eventually realized in 1945. While the parish priest at the time was proclaimed for having succeeded in getting the breakwater, it was in fact due to my father's relentless efforts over many years.

(27) John Henry Newman (1801- 1890) was an English cardinal and leader in the Oxford movement. Ordained in the Church of England in 1824, he eventually becoming vicar of St. Mary's, Oxford. In 1832, he resigned his position and went on a Mediterranean tour, during which he wrote many hymns, including *Lead Kindly Light*. His thoughts turned to Roman Catholicism and in 1841 he outraged Anglicans by attempting to demonstrate that their 39 articles were consistent with Roman Catholicism. He was received into the Catholic Church in 1845 and went to Rome

where he joined the Oratorian Order. Back in England, he became one of the most influential Catholics of all time. He and the English cardinal, Edward Manning, disagreed on many matters, especially the annunciation of the dogma of Papal infallibility. When the dust settled in 1879, he was made a cardinal and universally revered at the time of his death.

(28) Lord Edward Fitzgerald (1763-1798), a great Irish patriot, fought in the American Revolution as an officer in the British Army, from which he was expelled for his republican ideas. Back in Ireland he joined Wolfe Tone as a member of the United Irishmen. Together they led the Irish Rebel Uprising of 1798. Betrayed and captured, he was imprisoned at Newgate prison by the British, where he died of wounds. His wife, Lady Pamela Fitzgerald, was born illegitimate at Fogo, Newfoundland. The story of how she got from Fogo to being mistress of Leinster House, now the Irish Parliament, is told in my book *Breakers* (Breakwater Books, 1982, p. 61). As a child, she was adopted by the family of the Duke of Orleans. With the coming of the French Revolution, the family fled to England, where she met and married Lord Edward.

(29) Theobald Wolfe Tone (1763-1798) spent some time in France before becoming involved in rebellion in Ireland. He fostered several abortive expeditions from France to Ireland, and in 1798 was a leader of the United Irishmen's Rebellion with Lord Edward Fitzgerald. Defeated and captured by the English, Wolfe Tone was condemned to hang as a traitor, but insisted he was a soldier and should be shot. When this request was refused, he slit his throat with a pen knife in his prison cell and died.

(30) Jeremiah O'Donovan Rossa (1831-1915) was business manager of the strident republican newspaper, *Irish People*. Arrested, he spent five years in English prisons. After his release, he went to the U.S. where he continued to write inflammatory articles in support of Irish independence. When he died in 1915, Rossa's body

NO NEED TO WEAR RUBBERS

was brought back to Dublin and given a funeral, which attracted a massive crowd. At his graveside in Glasniven Cemetery, Patrick Pearse gave the immortal funeral oration, which ended with the words, "The fools, the fools, the fools! They have left us our Fenian dead, and while Ireland holds these graves, Ireland unfree shall never be at peace."

(31) Michael Collins (1890-1922) was leader of Sinn Fein. He was famous for organizing guerilla warfare in Ireland, which caused the British to sue for peace. He joined Arthur Griffith in setting up the Irish Free State in 1921 and was assassinated by his Irish enemies in 1922. His story was told in the film *Michael Collins*, starring Liam Neeson and Julia Roberts.

(32) Henry Gratten (1746-1820) was an Irish statesman and patriot who fought and won his battle to have the Irish parliament freed from English government control. He gained for Catholics the right to vote (1792) and consent for them to sit in parliament. This latter right was overruled by King George III, encouraging the United Irishmen's rising of 1798.

(33) August 1, 1915 a 36-year-old Patrick Pearse, who founded St. Enda's, a bilingual private school in Dublin, gained national attention as an outstanding orator when he gave a famous graveside speech for O'Donovan Rossa. The following year Pearse, Sean MacDermott, Eamonn Ceannt and Thomas Clarke, who had formed a committee of the Irish Republican Brotherhood (IRB), planned an uprising in Dublin in September 1915, but had to cancel plans when MacDermott was arrested. At the time they had only 55 recruits.

The rebellion, re-set for Easter Sunday, April 23, became known as the Easter Rebellion. All rising plans appear to have gone wrong. Rebels under the command of Patrick Pearse seized the General Post Office (GPO) as their headquarters; however, hardly any fighting took place there. Curious crowds gathered on Easter Monday afternoon to read a proclamation issued from the GPO by seven members of the IRB; it meant little at the time, but in retrospect was the beginning of the Republic of Ireland. By Thursday, British troops began to shell the GPO, which went up in a mass of flames. Pearse, now president of the Provisional Government of the Irish Republic, surrendered.

All the leaders of the rebellion were arrested, tried by court martial and condemned to be shot to death in Kilmainham Jail. After the last of them, James Connolly, whose leg had been shattered by a bullet, was carried from his cell to his death, Asquith, the British Prime Minister, halted the executions. This saved the lives of Countess Markievicz, who afterwards became the first woman elected to Parliament in Ireland or England, and Eamon de Valera, who lived to rule over an Irish state much different from that for which Connolly had died. The bodies of Pearse and the other dead signers were brought to nearby Arbour Hill prison, where they were buried in quick lime.

(34) Cathal Burga, leading tactician and strategist of the Irish Republican Army after 1916, was elected first president of the Dáil. In 1918, he masterminded the formation of the IRA general headquarters staff, preparing the secret army for rebellion. In 1919, he devised the stunning escape of Eamon de Valera from Lincoln Gaol. His ability and efficiency became legendary. With the connivance of Michael Collins in 1919 to 1920, he began in earnest an undeclared war between the IRA and the British in Ireland

(35) Charles Stuart Parnell was, in his lifetime, one of the most powerful leaders Ireland ever knew. His death enshrined him in Irish literature and folklore, his praises having been sung by such people as James Joyce and W.B. Yeats. A man of complex contradictions and extraordinary character, his life ended in personal tragedy. He possessed fierce pride and absolute faith in his cause;

a Protestant in a land of Catholics, an aristocrat who depended on the support of ordinary people. Known as the uncrowned King of Ireland, his scandalous love affair with Mrs. Katharine O'Shea resulted in one of the most infamous divorce cases of the Victorian era. It spawned political intrigue, treachery and hypocrisy that brought down the most magnificent Irish hero of them all. That this could lead to the tragic fall of such a man is incomprehensible.

(36) On January 21, 1919, Dáil Eireann was established by the new Free State Government. It ratified the establishment of the Irish Republic and declared the independence of the nation from British rule. The Dáil, or parliament, consists of democratically elected representatives of the Irish people.

(37) Edward P. Maher was born in St. John's in 1903. He graduated from All Hallows, Dublin, at age 24 in 1927, where he was ordained. He served at Sacred Heart Parish in Placentia from the early 1930s, and was there in 1947 when invested as a Domestic Prelate or Monseigneur. He afterwards served St. Joseph's Parish in St. John's from 1952 until ill-health forced his resignation in 1957. Monseigneur Maher died in 1961, age 58. His fellow seminary student was no more fortunate. Augustine Gibbs, born in St. John's in 1900, was ordained at All Hallow's College, Dublin in 1926 and served as assistant priest to Father Pippy at St. Joseph's, Hoylestown. A grotto in memory of Father Pippy was erected by him in 1937. It still stands on Quidi Vidi Road. Later that year, Father Gibbs died suddenly at the age of 37 while on a visit to Ireland, and is buried at All Hallow's.

(38) Constance Gore-Booth Markievicz lived at *Lissadel*, an ocean-side estate in Sligo, with her sister Eva. Their home was frequented by prominent Protestant Anglo-Irish, such as the Nobel Prize winning poet William Butler Yeats, who made the house and daughters famous in his poem "Lissadel," where he referred

to them as "two girls, both beautiful, one a gazelle."

A.E. (George Russell) wrote of the two sisters, "Ah, my darlings you will have to fight and suffer; you must endure loneliness, the coldness of friends, the alienation of love..." From 1898 to 1900 the life of Constance was centred in Paris where she met Count Casimir Dunin-Markievicz, a Polish count from Zywotowka in the Ukraine, on the terrace of the Café Flore. He was a giant of a man, about two metres tall and six years her junior. On September 29, 1900, she became Countess Markievicz.

Constance, like Yeats' great love, the actress Maude Gonne, was fired with the ambition to become Ireland's Joan of Arc. It was Constance who actually achieved that ambition. Shouting from platforms at political meetings in Dublin and plotting rebellion, with her mentor James Connolly, of whom she wrote in a poem:

"You died for your country my hero love...To Ireland and you I have pledged my life..."

After the collapse of the 1916 rising and the arrest of its leaders, her sister Eva, an artist of repute, fought valiantly in England and Ireland for commutation of Constance's death sentence, which Prime Minister Asquith, acting on a recommendation of the court-martial "only because of her sex," granted. The Rebel Countess was then transferred to an English jail. Yeats praised her in poetry;

"You, brave on such a hope forlorn / who smiled through crack of shot and shell/...Here's to you Constance in your cell."

On her release, and return to Ireland, the Kingstown jetty was so crowded with cheering crowds that it almost collapsed. Work was given up and traffic diverted as she made her way by car through enraptured crowds to an overwhelming reception in Dublin. With the creation of the Irish Free State she became Minister of Labour in the government and a Roman Catholic as a final step in her identification with Ireland. She went on to found the Irish Boy Scouts. In 1926, a year after my father saw her in the Dáil Eireann, the Irish Parliament, she died.

(39) The Royal Liver Building, located on Water Street, Liverpool, Merseyside, is the most famous attraction on the Liverpool waterfront. It was completed in 1911.

(40) Arthur Pratt was the son of Reverend John Pratt, a clergyman from County Durham, England whose ministry took him to a number of communities in Newfoundland, where his forceful preaching and evangelical fervour led to his nickname "Fiery John Pratt." His children were daughters Charlotte, Eleanor and Florence and sons, Arthur, William, James (grandfather of artist, Christopher Pratt and architect, Philip Pratt), Calvert (Senator Pratt), and E.J. (Edwin) the noted Canadian poet. Arthur enlisted in the Newfoundland Regiment in World War I. He was among those listed as "wounded in action," but after anxious weeks it was discovered his injuries had not been critical. Colonel Nicholson, in his book *The Fighting Newfoundlander*, refers to him as "the poet of the Blue Puttees." Unlike the more serious poetry of his brother E.J., Art wrote doggerel, in which he took great glee. After the war, he remained in England in what his father called "the commercial life," married a woman name Maud and had four children.

(41) Mary (Aylward) McGrath and husband James M., were the parents of Dr. James M. McGrath who helped institute the Janeway Children's Hospital, while serving as Minister of Health in the Smallwood Government (1956-1971). In 1908, Min McGrath, as she was known – who had a seriously handicapped small daughter, Margaret – decided to provide her with a legacy by opening Osborne Hotel on the upstairs floors of a shop on Water Street

directly opposite the General Post Office. The venture, financed with help from Sir Michael Cashin, was named for Osborne House, a favourite retreat of Queen Victoria and Prince Albert on the Isle of Wight. Because of its central location in the city, the hotel was very popular with outport visitors. My father sometimes stayed there when in St. John's on business. After little Margaret died at the age of 10, Osborne House had become so successful that Mrs. McGrath decided to keep it in operation. Around 1923, she leased the hotel to another woman, while retaining ownership of the place. Her granddaughter, author Robin McGrath, suggests that when my father met her in the saloon of the SS *Sachem* she was probably returning from a visit she made around that time to her son, James, the future Newfoundland Minister of Health, who was studying medicine in Dublin, Ireland, at National University.

BIBLIOGRAPHY

Abels, Jules. *The Parnell Tragedy*. Toronto: Macmillan Company, 1966.

Anderson, James. *The Harper Dictionary of Opera & Operetta*. London: Harper Collins, 1990.

Atkinson, Brooks. *Broadway*. New York: Macmillan Publishing Co., Inc., 1974.

Blimienes, Paulion, Sebastian Barrufet, Alfredo Villaverde. Barcelona. Turespaña, Spain: Ministerio de Estado de Comerdo, 2000.

Bridgewater, William. *The Columbia-Viking Desk Encyclopedia*. New York: Viking Press,1953.

Coogan, Tim Pat. *Eamon De Velera : The Man Who Was Ireland*. New York: Harper Collins,1996.

Cusack, Mary Frances. *An Illustrated History of Ireland: from AD 400 to 1800*. London: Bracken Books, Studio Editions Ltd.,1995.

Fleming, James M. *Roman Catholic Priests in Newfoundland*. History. Seattle, Washington: Self-published, 1998.

Keir, David. *The Bowring Story*. London: The Bodley Head, 1962.

Marreco, Anne. *The Rebel Countess*. New York: Chilton Books, 1967.

O' Neill, Paul. *The Oldest City: The Story of St. John's, Newfoundland*. Portugal Cove-St. Philip's, NL: Boulder Publications, 2003.

Pitt, David G. *E.J. Pratt: The Truant Years 1882-1927*. Toronto: University of Toronto Press, 1984.

Poole, Cyril (Editor). *Encyclopedia of Newfoundland and Labra-*

dor. Volume IV. St. John's, NL: Harry Cuff Publications Limited, 1993.

Ranelagh, John O'Beirne. *A Short History of Ireland*. Cambridge: Cambridge University Press, 1995.

Smith, John M. and Tim Cakwell. *The World Encyclopedia of Film*. New York: Galahad Books, 1972.

Story, G.M., W.J. Kirwin and J.D.A. Widdowson. *Dictionary of Newfoundland English*. Toronto: University of Toronto Press, 1982.

Warrack, John and Ewan West. *The Oxford Dictionary of Opera*. Oxford. Oxford University Press,1992.

INTERNET SOURCES

BIG BERTHA. www.nationmaster.com/encyclopedia/paris-gun-collections.ic.gc.ca/naismith/james/chronicles/chapter17r.htm

MISTINGUETT. www.geocities.com/_jimlowe/mist/mistdex.html

IDA RUBENSTEIN. www.michaelminn.net/andros/biographies/rubenstein-ida.htm

WALTER RUMMEL. www.scarecrowpress.com/catalog/ Prince of Virtuosos: A Life of Walter Rummel, American Pianist. By Charles Timbrell

SELFRIDGES. www.selfridges.co.uk